Twayne's English Authors Series

Sylvia E. Bowman, *Editor*

INDIANA UNIVERSITY

Dylan Thomas

(TEAS) 20

Dylan Thomas

By JACOB KORG

University of Washington

Twayne Publishers, Inc. :: New York

Copyright © 1965 by Twayne Publishers, Inc.

All Rights Reserved

Library of Congress Catalog Card Number: 64-8333

MANUFACTURED IN THE UNITED STATES OF AMERICA

Preface

Dylan Thomas has in common with the great poets the development of a unique poetic style. It is not a style congenial to all tastes; the criticism has been made that his subject matter is slight and that his means of expressing it is unnecessarily complicated and obscure. When a poetic construction is called a "Dylanism," we understand that it is considered inflated and pretentious. But a term used to reproach an imitator may constitute a tribute to the distinctiveness of the master. Both Thomas' distinction and the critical objections to his verse rest upon the fact that his poetry attempts to make the most, rhetorically, of common spiritual convictions. It almost offers an occasion for reopening the old debate about the primacy of thought and language as the source of myths, for it seeks to discover in the sleeping powers of language confirmations of ancient mystic universals.

This study attempts to observe Thomas at this work by tracing certain themes, tropes, and stylistic features. It opens with a brief biographical sketch, and then undertakes a general analysis of his style; these are followed by surveys of his verse, fiction, and dramatic works. Naturally, the greatest emphasis is placed on his poetry. In discussing it, I have brought forward some of its elements of unity and consistency; followed its development; placed individual poems; and, when coherence seemed to be in question, I have offered explications.

I wish to apologize in advance for certain deficiencies of critical tact that may be noted, with the excuse that they are imposed by requirements of space and readability. It has been impossible to supply illustrative quotations as often as necessary; I have been compelled to assume that the reader will be willing to consult Thomas' own text in connection with the detailed analyses. (The text used for the poems is the New Directions edition of *Collected Poems*, Sixteenth Printing; for the fiction, *Adventures in the Skin Trade and Other Stories*, New Directions.) I have often had to proceed to my conclusions rather abruptly, without fully sharing my way of reaching them with the reader. Those who know the intricacies of Thomas' craftsmanship will appreciate my motives for doing this. For the same reason, I have had to bypass much of interest that could be said about individual poems, limiting myself to their most prominent features. I have also silently had to acknowledge that the poetry of mysticism is most impervious to analysis when it is most successful.

Readers who have followed the growth of Thomas criticism will realize that I have made some effort to avoid duplicating earlier studies and that I am at the same time deeply indebted to them. So much of value has been written on Thomas that many of the poems have accumulated extensive bodies of commentary. It has not been feasible to give this material as much attention as it deserves in the text, but the bibliography is intended to render some acknowledgment of the use I have made of it. However, I should like to express a special indebtedness to the following, for the text does not reflect the full extent of my reliance on them:

"The Poetry of Dylan Thomas" by David Aivaz, *Hudson Review*, 1950; "The Wisdom of Poetry" by William Arrowsmith, *Hudson Review*, 1954; *A Casebook on Dylan Thomas*, edited by John Malcolm Brinnin, and Brinnin's *Dylan Thomas in America; A Key to Modern British Poetry* by Lawrence Durrell; *Entrances to Dylan Thomas' Poetry* by Ralph Maud; *The Poetry of Dylan Thomas* by Elder Olson; *Dylan Thomas, a Bibliography* by J. Alexander Rolph; *Dylan Thomas: The Legend and the Poet* edited by E. W. Tedlock, Jr.; and *A Reader's Guide to Dylan Thomas* by William Y. Tindall.

It is a pleasure also to acknowledge the assistance of the Lockwood Memorial Library at the University of Buffalo, which made microfilms of its Thomas manuscripts available, and that of Constantine FitzGibbon, Ralph Maud, Callum Mill, and Vernon Watkins.

Permission to quote from Thomas' publications has been granted by Dover Publications; Faber and Faber, Ltd; New Directions; and Yale University Press.

Preface

Lines from Robert Frost's "Once by the Pacific" are reprinted by permission of Holt, Rinehart & Winston, Inc. A passage from W. H. Auden's "September 1, 1939" is reprinted by permission of Random House. I am indebted to the Research Fund of the Graduate School of the University of Washington for a grant of funds to cover the expense of typing the manuscript of this book.

University of Washington   JACOB KORG
June, 1964

Contents

Chronology

1914   October 22, Dylan Thomas born at Swansea.

1925- Swansea Grammar School.
1931

1931- Worked as journalist for *Herald of Wales* and *South*
1932   *Wales Evening Post,* writing articles on literature and theater.

1933   May 18, published a poem in a London periodical for the first time, (An early version of "And death shall have no dominion," in *New English Weekly*.) September 3, the first of his poems appeared in the *Sunday Referee*. ("That sanity be kept")

1934   March 15, first short story, "After the Fair," published in *New English Weekly*. April, won *Sunday Referee* Book Prize for poetry. November, moved to London. December, publication of *18 Poems*.

1936   September, publication of *Twenty-five Poems*.

1937   July 12, married to Caitlin Macnamara in Penzance.

1938   Moved to Laugharne.

1939   January, son, Llewelyn, born. August, publication of *The Map of Love*.

1940   April, publication of *Portrait of the Artist as a Young Dog*.

1941   August, Moved to London, began to work for British Broadcasting Corporation as script writer and reader, and to write film scripts.

1943   February, Publication of *New Poems*, Daughter, Aeron, born.

1946   February 7, publication of *Deaths and Entrances*. November 8, publication of *Selected Writings*.

1948   Moved to the Boat House, Laugharne.

1949   Son, Colm, born.

1950   February-May, first American reading tour.

1952 January-May, second American tour, accompanied by Caitlin. February 28, publication of *In Country Sleep*. November 10, publication of *Collected Poems*. (By the time of the eighth impression, January, 1955, 30,800 copies had been published.)

1953 March 31, American edition of *Collected Poems* published. April-June, third American tour. May 14, publication of *The Doctor and the Devils*. October, left England for the United States. November 9, died in New York.

CHAPTER 1

Biographical

I

DYLAN THOMAS' life and times have only a limited relevance to his poetry. It is particularly clear from his early poems, where, as Marc Alyn has observed, all of his originality is already on view, that he was occupied with introspections that lie outside of time and place, and that his style owes comparatively little to tradition or to example. These poems do contain an occasional obscure allusion to the environment in which they were written, such as Cwmdonkin Park, where Thomas played as a child, and the "waste allotments" of Swansea. In addition, much of his prose is autobiographical, and his later poems often take as their points of departure the people and places of South Wales; but these lose their identity as they are transformed into the material of Thomas' world. His verse is said to resemble the intricate Welsh forms in spirit, if not in detail; and his mysticism probably owes something to regional folklore. But there is comparatively little about Thomas and his experiences that can help us in understanding his poetry. In fact, apart from occasional glancing correspondences of pose and manner, it is difficult to see any meaningful relation between Thomas' hieratic, disciplined verse and the earthy, disorganized Welshman who wrote it. He seems to have reserved all his faculties for his poetry and to have conducted his life as if it were an afterthought.

Thomas has described his childhood as that of a perfectly ordinary, dirty, mischievous, and adventuresome street urchin. His father, David J. Thomas, was Senior English master at the Swansea Grammar School, which Dylan attended; and English was the only subject in which the boy escaped mediocrity. He began to contribute good verses to the school magazine at the age of eleven. The mock radio broadcasts and the game of writing alternate lines of poems described by Daniel Jones[1] are boyish expressions of the wit, exuberant imagination, and passion for words that many of Thomas' early friends have mentioned. The profound impression he created as a reader of poetry at the height of his career was anticipated by an adolescent acting flair, for he had leading roles in school and in little theater productions from time to time between the ages of sixteen and twenty. His experiences with nature took place during visits to the seashore and to his aunt's farm in Carmarthenshire. The aunt, Ann Jones, and her farm, which Thomas called "Fern Hill," are, of course, the subjects of two of his finest poems; and both appear also in "The Peaches," "The Gardener," and other prose writings.

After leaving grammar school at seventeen in 1931, Thomas worked as a writer on books, theatricals, and other cultural subjects for the weekly *Herald of Wales* and as a reporter for the *South Wales Evening Post.* Also, as is clear from the stories in *Portrait of the Artist as a Young Dog,* he spent much time exploring the streets, pubs, and alleys of the depression-ridden seaport town, sharing the frustrations of an impoverished provincial generation. The short stories give impressive pictures of the external conditions of Thomas' life at this time, but the record of his poetic development is contained in the penny exercise books in which he used to write his poems. These notebooks—dated between 1930 and 1934 and now in the Lockwood Memorial Library at the University of Buffalo—contain numerous rejected poems and drafts from which published versions of poems were derived. They suggest also the spiritual crises Thomas was experiencing between the ages of sixteen and twenty. The nature of these trials is obscure; they seem to be related to love affairs, to industrial civilization, and to the familiar youthful problem of finding one's identity. As he groped among painful and oppressive feelings, turning his thoughts into poems, Thomas was formulating both a mysticism and a poetic style.

The Buffalo notebooks reveal that Thomas had already written much of his best and most original poetry before he was twenty. They show that thirteen of the *18 Poems* were written before April, 1934; that half of the *Twenty-five Poems* were printed from versions completed as early as 1933; and that some were revisions, made early in 1936, of drafts written in 1933.[2] Thomas was to write more finished, more elaborate, and certainly more compassionate poems later in his career; but they can only be regarded as extensions of the highly original poetic idiom he fashioned when, as a schoolboy and as a loose-ends juvenile reporter, he neglected his duties in order to twist his private discoveries of the paradoxes of existence into arcane, eccentric, and highly organized verse. This is the period Thomas was referring to when he said to Harvey Breit in a 1950 interview: "Then I was arrogant and lost. Now I am humble and found. I prefer that other."[3]

For a number of years after Thomas' death it was thought that the London publication of his poems had begun with the appearance of "That sanity be kept" in the *Sunday Referee* of September 3, 1933, and "No man believes who, when a star falls shot" in the *Adelphi* of September 6. But Ralph Maud has discovered that an early version of "And death shall have no dominion" had been published in the *New English Weekly* of May 18, 1933.[4] However, it was not until September that Thomas began to place a poem nearly every month in one of the respectable London periodicals, such as the *Adelphi,* the *New English Weekly,* and the *Listener.* Geoffrey Grigson reports that after Stephen Spender had called his attention to Thomas' contributions to the "Poet's Corner" of the *Sunday Referee,* he wrote to suggest that he submit some of his poems to *New Verse;* and he published a number of them, beginning with "Our eunuch dreams" in April, 1934.

The publication of Thomas' first volume of verse, *18 Poems,* came about in the following way. Victor Neuburg, poetry editor of the *Sunday Referee,* who had accepted a number of Thomas' early poems for his "Poet's Corner" toward the end of 1933, had recently begun the practice of giving awards to the authors of the best poems appearing there in each six-month period. The award consisted of the publication of a volume of poems in a *Sunday Referee* Poets Series. On April 22, 1934, the newspaper announced that Thomas' "The force that through the green fuse," which had appeared on October 29, 1933, was the winner of the second of these prizes. Thomas' volume was delayed as the publisher originally chosen for it hesitated to bring it out, but David Archer, owner of the Parton Bookshop, who had seen Thomas' manuscript poems, agreed to publish it at his own expense. Ultimately, *18 Poems* was published jointly by the *Sunday Referee* and the Parton Bookshop in the middle of December, 1934; the first edition of the forty-page volume consisted of two hundred and fifty copies, and it was met with nearly absolute silence by the reviewers and the press.

Throughout 1934 and 1935, Thomas published poems, short stories, and reviews in the *Adelphi,* the *Herald of Wales,* the *Sunday Referee, New Verse,* the *Criterion,* and other periodicals. Perhaps it was as a result of this encouragement, as well as his talk with Grigson, and the *Sunday Referee* Book Prize, that Thomas moved to London in late 1934. He seems to have been unemployed at this time, and he certainly felt oppressed by Swansea's provincialism and lack of opportunity. He came to London without any definite prospects, but with the intention, as an autobiographical character in a later story says, of living as a free-lance journalist, or "on women."

Just how he did live is not clear, but the poems appearing in periodicals found their admirers, and Thomas became known to many of the writers then living in London. The nineteen or twenty-year-old Thomas has been described by Roy Campbell, Lawrence Durrell, Pamela Hansford Johnson, and others as a slight, curly-haired, shy provincial, an excellent tapside mimic and wit, who was often to be seen working over exercise books of his poems in pubs, with a glass of beer beside him. Though he soon gained greater confidence, his acquaintances noticed that he was easily intimidated by the prospect of encountering new people and situations and that he had a peasantlike aversion to the unfamiliar. Whether he was in Florence, in New York, or in an American college town, he preferred drinking with a friend in a bar to seeing the sights and to meeting well-known writers or foreign intellectuals. He was not curious about literature. Though he knew much about his contemporaries among the poets and wrote excellent book reviews, he was, in general, no more than a casual reader with a preference for detective stories. On the other hand, he was reported to be quite serious about his skill at the time-killing pub game of shove-ha'penny, and he enjoyed such homely entertainments as Monopoly and

Ludo. He had, as Daniel Jones said, "discerned clearly and from the beginning the things that were of no use to him," and he made no effort to come to terms with them.[5] This absorption in himself and in his work made him appear to various observers to be shy, egotistic, irresponsible, selfish, or arrogant.

One of the first tributes to his talent came from Edith Sitwell, who, in February, 1936, praised "A grief ago," which had recently appeared in a periodical, saying that it represented a great advance upon *18 Poems*.[6] She also wrote a highly favorable review in the London *Sunday Times* of *Twenty-five Poems* when it appeared in September of that year. This second volume was the result of a suggestion by Victor Neuburg, who told Thomas that he should not delay too long before publishing another book. Thomas quickly presented him with the contents of a new volume, consisting of some poems which had already been published in periodicals and of others drawn from the manuscripts he was continually working on. Through the agency of Runia Sheila MacLeod, *Twenty-five Poems* was published by the firm of J. M. Dent; and, unlike *18 Poems*, this book attracted some critical attention.

Unlike most of his contemporaries among the poets, Thomas was not a university man from a wealthy family, a radical, or a citizen of the world. In spite of a brief flirtation with Marxism and a naïve, passionate sympathy with all poor people, he was not interested in social problems; he hated academics and academicism, and had no taste for discussions of art and literature. The fact that he won the admiration of such people as Herbert Read, Edith Sitwell, Stephen Spender and Lawrence Durrell without having had the usual advantages is the strongest possible tribute to his native talent. He could not, of course, be classed with the Auden group, and many early critics assigned him to Surrealism, the new manner emerging at nearly the same time as his first books of poems. *Contemporary Poetry and Prose,* a periodical hospitable to Surrealist and related writing, and edited by Thomas' friend, Roger Roughton, carried his short story, "The Burning Baby," and two of his poems in its first issue in May, 1936. Thomas also took part in one of the Surrealist exhibitions of that year. It was natural for Surrealism and the other neo-Romantic tendencies to attach themselves to him, for he was the strongest exponent of the principles they supported. But he was clearly independent of any influence they might have exerted.

At first, Thomas' readers believed that his near-incoherent poetry was the result of a spontaneous, uncritical outpouring of language. But it has since become clear that each of his poems is an exhaustively calculated construction. He once said, in reply to a question asked at the University of Utah, that he worked on his poems for months and years. Lawrence Durrell discovered with surprise that Thomas wrote slowly and painfully, trying the words in many forms, and that he once filled a whole exercise book with variants of a single phrase. In later years, his practice did not change; there are 143 work sheets in the manuscript of "Poem on His Birthday" at the Harvard University Library; and John Malcolm Brinnin reported that Thomas once showed him over two hundred separate drafts of "Fern Hill." The fact that Thomas wrote only six poems in the last six years of his life did not mean that he was idle, but that he was carrying his usual working method to an extreme.

Apparently, Thomas usually began a poem with a phrase he found suggestive, and then added to it through links of sound, imagery, and association. Though this process was carried on intuitionally, and with little attention to intelligibility, it was obviously subject to firm intellectual control. Thomas usually adopted demanding forms, with clear rhyme schemes and intricate stanzas, and wrote in syllabic verse, in which each syllable was accounted for. "Vision and Prayer" is perhaps the most extreme example of his characteristic formal discipline. Further, there are persistent suggestions in Thomas' remarks about his poetry that his intuitions were kept in order by strict, if obscure, determinants of sense. He once wrote to Vernon Watkins that the poems he was working on were illogical, "except by a process it's too naturally obvious to misexplain."[7]

The accumulation of a poem about its point of origin was so close to being systematic that John Malcolm Brinnin gained the impression from Thomas that it was like a geometrical demonstration in which the poem could be "proven" on the basis of what was "given." So clearly was the rest of the poem suggested by the word or phrase that generated it that Thomas often

felt he knew in advance the place it would occupy in the un-
written poem.[8] His feeling that a poem should be strictly ordered
appears in his objection that a poem sent to him for criticism
had ". . . none of the strong, inevitable pulling that makes a
poem an event, a happening, an action. . . ."[9] Differing with
the Surrealist view of poetry, he said: "I do not mind from
where the images of a poem are dragged up; drag them up,
if you like, from the nethermost sea of the hidden self; but,
before they reach paper, they must go through all the rational
processes of the intellect."[10]

II

Thomas had first met Caitlin Macnamara, his future wife, at
a party in London, but they grew interested in each other on
the occasion which has been described by the painter, Augustus
John.[11] John had brought Caitlin, who was sitting for him as
a model, to stay at the house of Richard Hughes in Laugharne;
there they met Thomas, who was also visiting Hughes, while pre-
paring to go for a drive through the countryside. Thomas joined
them in their car, and John's account suggests that the courtship
began immediately with considerable momentum in the back
seat. Thomas and Caitlin were married in July, 1937, in Penzance and, as Thomas wrote, "with no money, no prospect of
money, no attendant friends or relatives, and in complete happiness. We've been meaning to from the first day we met.
. . ."[12] After extended visits with Caitlin's family in Ringwood,
Hampshire, and with Thomas' family in Bishopston near Swansea, they moved to Laugharne, where Richard Hughes had offered them his house, in the middle of 1938. The quaint and
remote little fishing village became their permanent home, but
they frequently lived at other places in and out of Wales during
World War II. Thomas' time of settling in Laugharne coincides
roughly with the period when his poetry began to turn outward;
his love for Caitlin, the birth of his first child, Llewelyn, re-
sponses to the Welsh countryside and its people, and ultimately
events of the war began to enter his poetry as visible subjects.

Between his marriage and 1941, when he moved to London,
Thomas wrote most of *The Map of Love* and *Deaths and En-*

trances, as well as the stories in *Portrait of the Artist as a Young Dog*. He continued to place poems and stories in magazines, and he had two volumes published. All this was accomplished, however, in the face of absolute poverty. At this time, he became a master of the begging letter. He wrote frequently to Vernon Watkins and others to complain of his penury and to ask for money; and he was grateful for gifts as small as a half-crown. When his friend, Keidrych Rhys, the editor of *Wales*, was to be married, Thomas wrote to Watkins to ask whether he could borrow a suit for the occasion; when he was sent one as a gift, he mustered up a little comic performance to thank him for it.

Within a month after the outbreak of the war, Thomas had decided to register as a conscientious objector. However, this never became necessary because a weakness in his chest caused him to be rejected for military service. In 1940 he, Caitlin, and Llewelyn moved to John Davenport's house in Wiltshire, where an irregular wartime household of artists, musicians, and writers waiting to be called to military assignments had assembled. In August, 1941, Thomas wrote to Watkins that he and Caitlin had made a desperate penniless march on London, leaving Llewelyn behind with his grandmother, and were despondently awaiting some improvement in their situation. "Soon perhaps this will have been worn away, hunger, anger, boredom, hate and unhappiness. . . . We are prisoners now in a live melodrama and all the long villains with three half-pence are grinning in at us through the bars."[13] It must have been shortly after this letter that Dylan and Caitlin met Roy Campbell, who was then serving as an air-raid warden, and the two poets made a tour of acquaintances to borrow money. Their only success came when they intruded upon T. S. Eliot, who gave them enough to tide them over until both secured radio jobs.

After this, Thomas became relatively prosperous. He lived in London during the war, and his work for the British Broadcasting Corporation, both as a scriptwriter and a reader of poetry on the Third Programme, led him to think of writing radio plays, detective stories, film scripts, and other popular forms. Whether this activity interfered with his poetry is an open question. Some of his best poems, including "The Marriage of a Virgin," and "Vision and Prayer" date from the war years, and

the experiences of the war had the double effect of providing
him with subjects for such poems as "A Refusal to Mourn" and
of stimulating the altruistic element of his later work. *The Doctor and the Devils, Under Milk Wood,* and *The Beach at
Falesá* clearly have their origins in the public communication
media with which Thomas was working at this time.

Partly as a result of his work with the British Broadcasting
Corporation and partly because of the popularity of *Portrait of
the Artist as a Young Dog,* Thomas was known to a much wider
public after the war. In 1948 he returned to Laugharne, renting
the Boat House, which has since become identified with him.
This is a small, three-storied structure perched above a seawall on
a cliff over Laugharne Bay. About a hundred yards along the
cliff is a small shack where Thomas worked. The atmosphere
and details of Laugharne, including the deserted Laugharne
Castle with its tower, had appeared in earlier stories and poems;
and they were now more steadily observed in such poems as
"Over Sir John's hill." He continued to do broadcasting and
film work after the war, and was reported to be earning an
excellent income; but his management of his money was so
poor that the household remained penniless, and he was continually in debt. He was now a well-known literary figure as a
result of his books published on both sides of the Atlantic, his
radio readings, and the respect with which literary people
approached his poetry. The consequence was that he was invited by John Malcolm Brinnin to come to America in February,
1950, for the first of his reading tours.

These last years of Thomas' life, which have little to do with
his poetry but which made him known as a personality and
phenomenon to a huge American public, have been covered in
Brinnin's *Dylan Thomas in America.* During his three American
tours Thomas had to travel across the country giving readings,
usually at college campuses. At each stop he encountered people
unknown to him who might meet him with hostility or fatuous
adulation, and he was subjected to a hodgepodge of dinners,
cocktail parties, receptions, and panel discussions. The experience was a mixture of things he liked—such as pretty women,
drinks, admiration and attention—and of those he detested, such
as academic formality and strange people and places.

It was not long before Brinnin, who had generously undertaken to plan Thomas' tours, found that, like Dr. Frankenstein, he had unleashed an unpredictable form of life on the country's campuses. Thomas, who was still fundamentally shy and timorous, was easily disturbed by the unfamiliar. Further, during his depression-ridden youth and the impromptu living of the war years in Bohemian digs in Chelsea and Laugharne, he had grown accustomed to considerable freedom from inhibition. His behavior in America was the result of a combination of terror and bravado; he had the chance to use whatever defenses he pleased against the unfamiliar, such as rudeness and drunkenness, with the added satisfaction that he was enlivening the spectacle he was expected to provide.

It is also clear, however, that he was not his own master, but was driven by disturbances that had become chronic long before he came to America. Though he could not be intentionally unkind, and suffered intense remorse at the pain he caused others, his irresponsibility nevertheless spread embarrassment, confusion, and concern among his friends. Brinnin found that Thomas would neither eat nor sleep unless compelled to, that he drank incessantly and foolishly, spent his money with complete indifference, and was subject to unpredictable changes of mood, including profound depressions. His anecdotes about Thomas pursuing women at parties, using profanity with students and faculty members, and vomiting in the street are only among the most reliable examples of a vast lore about the poet that sprang up on the dozens of campuses across the country where he was seen. The three series of readings and the final three weeks in New York just before his death were a sort of macabre royal progress combining the triumphant, the pathetic, the ludicrous, and, of course, the tragic.

Thomas, who had come to America to earn badly needed money, actually made several thousands on his first tour, but he went back to England with only eight hundred dollars. Not long after Thomas and Caitlin arrived for the second tour, they suddenly ran out of money; Brinnin found that they had been spending a hundred dollars a day, and that they could not account for it. Before the end of this tour it was learned that Llewelyn had been dropped from his school because Thomas, in spite of several warnings, had failed to send his tuition fee in time. In Washington, when Thomas was invited to stay at the luxurious home of Francis Biddle, the former Attorney-General of the United States, he felt impelled by some obscure revolutionary motive to steal a number of shirts from a drawer as he left. He freely confessed his crime to Brinnin, but he refused to return the stolen goods. He once borrowed a raincoat from the poet Richard Eberhart and failed to return it; instead, some time later and after he had gone back to Wales, he made a futile gesture of reparation by sending, as a replacement, an old, worn coat of his own which was too small for Eberhart. Once, while he was traveling between two engagements in Michigan in a car, his companions smelled smoke; it turned out that Thomas' clothes had caught fire from a cigarette butt he had dropped into his pocket.

In spite of the disturbances Thomas caused, the purpose of his visit to America was abundantly fulfilled. He became known to a whole generation of American readers and poets; and, as Brinnin emphasized, he missed only one out of a hundred and fifty engagements, though he was often late. His readings were so successful that they can only be called charismatic; he both shed and gathered strength through them. Thomas' qualities, whatever they were, transfixed his audiences and opened them to the evocative power of the spoken word as no other performer could. His recordings convey the essentials of his manner. He read in a sort of rhythmic intonation, mouthing every vowel and consonant heavily in a sustained, full-throated tone. This style, we are given to understand, is a counterpart of the incantatory *hwyl* characteristic of Welsh preachers. Thomas paid little attention to expression or variety of emphasis, as if recognizing that the intonations of actual speech were not appropriate to his poetry. He was not quite so effective as a reader of the work of other poets; it seemed as if his reading style and his own verse were best suited to each other.

Since Thomas spent what he earned immediately, his American reading tours did not relieve his financial situation. When Brinnin visited him in Wales, he found him hemmed in by all sorts of difficulties: his relations with Caitlin were stormy, he did not like living either at the Boat House or in London, he had failed to fulfill a writing commitment for which he had accepted an advance, and, most disturbing of all, he lacked the confidence for continuing with his writing. Under these circumstances, he welcomed the invitations to America as a means of escaping mounting pressures. Brinnin's account of his dangerous and uncontrolled behavior just before his death in the fall of 1953 after he had come to America for the fourth time, strongly suggest that physical and psychological disasters were irresistibly approaching Thomas. He had grown increasingly aware of a constant feeling of terror that he could escape only by drinking, yet this means of escape was now beginning to fail him, for he could not drink without becoming sick. He was at the point of physical collapse. Though he had to spend some time in bed during these last three weeks and occasionally seemed to suffer alarming hallucinations, *Under Milk Wood* was revised, rehearsed, and performed; and there were the usual parties and readings.

Then, one day, while he was being nursed through one of his fits of illness, exhaustion, and remorse by the woman Brinnin calls "Liz," Thomas announced that he was going out for a drink. He returned to boast that he had downed eighteen straight whiskies. He fell asleep. On the following day he lapsed into unconsciousness. After lying in a coma for four days at St. Vincent's Hospital, he died. He had, in effect, killed himself; the massive dose of alcohol he had taken had caused cerebral poisoning. His body was sent back to Laugharne, where he was buried in St. Martin's Churchyard, which overlooks the rolling fields near the town.

At his death, Thomas left unfinished *Adventures in the Skin Trade* and the poem titled "Elegy." But he was also planning to write the libretto for an operatic work with music by Igor Stravinsky. The two had discussed this project at a meeting in Boston earlier in 1953, and Thomas' autumn trip had been intended to take him to California in order to spend some time working with the composer. The opera was to be about a couple who have somehow survived the destruction of all life on earth and are witnessing its reappearance. As they encounter familiar natural phenomena for the first time, they also recreate language, culture, and myth. They relive the first experiences of the human race. The music for this libretto was to be in a style resembling *Le Sacre du Printemps,* and the landscape where the events take place would be anthropomorphic, reflecting primitive notions of nature. In a 1950 broadcast, Thomas had mentioned a similar subject as the theme of a projected long poem to be called "In Country Heaven." He described "In Country Sleep," "Over Sir John's hill," and "In the White Giant's Thigh" as parts of this longer work. It is clear that the opera he was planning at the end of his life was intended, like the uncompleted poem, to be a paradoxical "affirmation of the beautiful and terrible worth of the Earth."[14]

CHAPTER 2

The Rhetoric of Mysticism

I

THOMAS' love of poetry began, not with ideas, but with words. In answering some questions about his writing, he reported that, as a child, he had been attracted by the sounds of the words in nursery rhymes, but had paid little attention to their meanings: "The words, 'Ride a cock-horse to Banbury Cross' were . . . haunting to me, who did not know then what a cock-horse was nor cared a damn where Banbury Cross might be. . . ."[1] Language seemed not to refer to the real world but to generate through its sounds intimate new realities which the child could appropriate as his own: "And these words were, to me, as the notes of bells, the sounds of musical instruments, the noises of the wind, sea, and rain, the rattle of milkcarts, the clopping of hooves on cobbles, the fingering of branches on a window pane, might be to someone deaf from birth, who has miraculously found his hearing."[2]

When he decided to become a writer, Thomas' attitude toward words was "The first thing was to feel and know their sound and substance; what I was going to do with those words, what use I was going to make of them, what I was going to *say* through them, would come later."[3] This emphasis on the reality of words themselves continued when he became aware of their magic capacity for referring to the qualities and sensations of life.

Because the passion for words is the root of his poetic style, the rhetorical resources of sound, imagery, and structured language found in Thomas' poems assert their authority over the feelings without much support from detachable meaning. Nevertheless, one of the important problems Thomas faced was that of finding themes appropriate to the imaginative use of words as he understood it. His early unpublished poems show that he secured such themes in the prelogical convictions about being and reality which came to him in the course of his efforts to solve the spiritual perplexities of his youth. These ideas are far from original. They are among the oldest and most elementary beliefs mankind has held, the irreducible truths that present themselves when the imagination pursues ultimate conclusions. However, great truths have the disadvantage of being truistic. When they are expressed in conventional language and through conventional rhetoric, they become inert and banal. But Thomas approached them through his own introspections and undertook to revitalize them through his "devious craftsmanship" of language. As a result, in his poetic idiom we sense the imaginative vision shaping the rhetoric, and the rhetoric adapting itself to the exceptional requirements of the vision. His style is controlled, ultimately, neither by his mysticism, nor by his joy in language; it is, at its best, a balanced collaboration between them.

The substance of Thomas' vision consists of a number of convictions about time, immortality, personal identity, the unity of existence, and similar matters which are the familiar principles of intuitive religion. The obscurities of the poems occupied with this vision are partly attributable to the limitations shared by all literature of mysticism, which are more stringent forms of the limitations of poetry in general. The spirit has no language of its own; language grows out of the need for communicating the familiar experiences of daily life, not those which are unique and ineffable. Language seems strangely bound by a conservative principle which dictates that it can tell only what the hearer already knows. Its usual course, when it has a new thing to say, is to resort to something familiar which resembles its own subject, and the practical device of analogy is a universal favorite among mystic writers.

As W. T. Stace has pointed out, all expressions of mystic insight must be figurative, for mystic truths are outside the field of literal meaning. ". . . any proposition asserting any relation between God and the world," says Stace, "is a symbolic proposition and not a literal truth."[4] The mystic writers themselves frequently warn us that the expressive resources available to them are inadequate to their subject; even when they use comparisons, these must be understood as "analogies of proportionality." The two terms of such analogies resemble each other in possessing some common attribute as in all analogies, but each possesses it in a way appropriate to itself, so that the attribute is not identical in both cases after all. For example, in speaking of God's "love" the mystic cannot mean something identical with human love, but he does not mean something entirely different from it: he means such love as God can be considered as having, and he is therefore using an indefinite expression whose meaning depends on something admittedly incommunicable, the nature of God.

Thus, even apocalyptic metaphor and mystical symbolism do not enable the mystic to escape the limitations of language or to pierce the wall of the inexpressible. They simply enable him to refer to the transcendental by referring, in the first instance, to a version of actual experience imaginatively reshaped for the purpose. In such imagery the natural world is penetrated with mystic reality, so that its ordinary values, appearances, and relationships are disrupted. What is called mysticism in literature has as its subject a mixed cosmos, a point of intersection between natural and supernatural orders. In this context language cannot maintain its conventional meanings; its terms are rendered ambiguous, twisted, and perverted, acquiring new possibilities of meaning, as in Rimbaud's *alchimie du verbe*. Thomas' idiom employs the derangement of language to express perceptions of the sort which Rimbaud described as accessible to a derangement of the senses. Religious writers working within established traditions may successfully exploit conventional symbols and terms. But the secular mystic must use language in ways that forestall a banal intelligibility and force the mind toward new ranges of meaning. For Thomas, as for Blake and Yeats, this entailed the development of a private symbology, a system of metaphor capable of expressing a visionary reality.

This chapter will describe Thomas' mysticism and its relationship to his use of language and imagery. But it should be observed that the style under consideration is found in its most characteristic form only in Thomas' early work. Modulations in poetic technique and changes in subject matter rendered the poems he wrote after *The Map of Love* far more accessible. The mythic consciousness from which the early poems emerge is never entirely left behind. But as Thomas became concerned with external experiences and with the problem of communication, the mythic consciousness gradually retreated into the background, so that in the later poems ultimate realities are approached through nature and daily life instead of visionary imagery. Critics have accounted for the changes in Thomas' work in a number of ways, usually dividing it into three overlapping stages. G. S. Fraser characterizes the second and third stages as marked by religious and human interests respectively, while the first has neither.[5] According to Elder Olson, Thomas moved from a "dark" phase occupied with private enigmas to expressions of strong feeling for others, and finally to a period when "faith and love" supplanted the painful emotions of the first two stages, as he found a way to God through man and nature.[6]

The universe which is both the subject and the setting of Thomas' early poetry and short stories is a rediscovery of the reality found in primitive religion. It is an arena of conflict between the forces of creation and destruction embodied in the processes of nature. Fertility, birth, death, growth, decay, and, in fact, all events are episodes of a war of processes which rages in every organism and every living cell. The energy driving these "impious systems"—as they are called in Thomas' short story, "The Holy Six"—manifests itself in the sexual urge, in the fertility of the soil, and in the lifegiving elements of water and sunlight. The seasons of the year, the unfolding of generations, and the alternations of life and death are stages in the dialectic drama of existence. This schematization of the biological processes yields the accurate, if elementary, insight that all things participate in all others because natural changes involve the constant shifting of particles of matter from one form of life to another. Thomas' early short stories often confirm the themes of his poems, and this vision of the continuity of nature is vividly described in the climactic nightmare of "The Visitor":

Now the sheep fell and the flies were at them. The rats and the weasels, fighting over the flesh, dropped one by one. . . . It was . . . but a little time before the dead, picked to the symmetrical bone, were huddled in under the soil by the wind that blew louder and harder as the fat flies dropped on to the grass. Now the worm and the death-beetle undid the fibres of the animal bones, worked at them brightly and minutely, and the weeds through the sockets and the flowers on the vanished breasts sprouted up with the colours of the dead life fresh on their leaves. And the blood that had flowed flowed over the ground, strengthening the blades of the grass, ful-filling the wind-planted seeds in its course, into the mouth of the spring. . . . He saw the streams and the beating water, how the flowers shot out of the dead, and the blades and roots were doubled in their power under the stride of the split [sic] blood.[7]

The unity of matter is paralleled by a unity of spiritual life. All nature is joined in one great brotherhood, so that the separate-ness and even the antagonism of individual creatures is merely a transient aspect of their essential identity with each other. This view of the universe as a seamless fabric is typical of the myth-making imagination. The primitive mind, says Cassirer, knows nothing of the distinctions scientific thinking has imposed upon experience:

Its view of life is a synthetic, not an analytic one. Life is not divid-ed into classes and subclasses. It is felt as an unbroken continuous whole which does not admit of any clean-cut and trenchant dis-tinction. . . . There is no specific difference between the various realms of life. Nothing has a definite, invariable, static shape. By a sudden metamorphosis everything may be turned into everything. If there is any characteristic and outstanding feature of the myth-ical world, any law by which it is governed—it is this law of meta-morphosis.[8]

Thomas' view that life and death are merely stages within the universal process is expressed in his first published poem, "And death shall have no dominion." The poem displays both a correspondence between Thomas' mysticism and conventional Christian doctrines, and his manner of departing from them in the direction of more primitive attitudes. The refrain, as Thomas E. Connolly has pointed out, is an echo of a verse from St. Paul's Epistle to the Romans where Paul argues that since baptism is a symbolic parallel for the death and resurrection of Christ, his hearers, who have been baptized, are free of the sin associated with death. Paul says of Jesus in passing that ". . . death hath no more dominion of him."[9] Thomas makes use of the same logic, and even of the same water symbolism, when he says of the dead, "Though they sink through the sea they shall rise again." However, he goes beyond the Christian framework thus established and toward a more general mysticism in envisioning the dead men as resurrected, not in a single deity, but in the elements of nature. Human immortality is thus a spiritual consequence of the unity of matter, for in Thomas' universe, as he says in some Blakean lines from the posthumous "Shiloh's Seed," "From the meadow where Lambs frolic,/Rises every blade the Lamb."[10]

A second condition of Thomas' universe, and one whose effects are indistinguishable from those of the unity of matter, is unity of time. As the mystic, in his attempt to grasp absolute reality, includes more and more of the cosmic scene in his vision he perceives that life and death recur in a more or less regular way; and they create, when the universe is seen as a whole, an impression of stability rather than change. Kenneth Burke's principle that the widening of the "circumference" of a context changes what is within it operates here, for *sub specie aeternitatis*, the alternations of life and death cease to oppose each other and become stages in a single process. The vicissitudes of the biological conflict are no more than consecutive conditions of the eternal life of the universe. Existence assumes the aspect of a single enduring fact whose changes are mere pulsations of the energy flowing through it, and time assumes the "mythopoeic" quality which Philip Wheelwright has described in this way:

. . . mythic time is felt to be cyclical, and therefore, in a way, recurrent. Each thing, or what may pass for it, has happened before and will happen again. Time spirals rather than marches. . . . the mythic idea of time sets up a relationship that is not serial but exemplifies . . . the tendency of events, perhaps remote if measured by historical standards, to coalesce on the basis of some similarity or felt congruity or recurrent tribal ritual. . . . Past, present, and future coalesce, and in place of the, to us, familiar lines of distinction between them the mythic attitude substitutes the ideas of Creation, Sacrament and Prophecy.[11]

The unity of time amounts, of course, to an absence of time. To the perfect vision of the mystic, time is neither an irresistibly passing stream nor a rigidly ordered and irreversible sequence; it is an eternal present. The world is in all stages of its development at once. Duration is laid out flat before the eye, like a map, so that the different conditions through which things pass are seen simultaneously, telescoped into a single composite entity. Birth and death, sin and redemption, growth and decline exist side by side, superimposed upon one another. There is no distinction between the potential and the actual.

In Thomas' view, the embryo is already the child, the man, and the corpse; the corpse, in turn, is the decomposed elements which will feed the plants and so be returned to the cycle of life and death. Events and conditions ordinarily regarded as sequential are concurrent, so that in "Before I knocked," the speaker of the poem, Jesus, can declare in speaking of the crucifixion, "As yet ungotten, I did suffer." Like the unity of matter, the unity of time renders all things participants in one another's existence. Polar opposites merge, so that ". . . the womb/Drives in a death as life leaks out," and "Light breaks where no sun shines." The innumerable paradoxes of Thomas' poetry are assertions of the harmony and unity which appear when the dialectic universe is freed from time: "I am the man your father was," "Over the past table I repeat this present grace," ". . . of my clay is made the hangman's lime." Thomas' explanation of his poetic method in a famous letter to Henry Treece shows that his characteristic rhetoric is an attempt to capture this vision of conflict and resolution: "Out of the inevitable conflict of images—inevitable because of the creative, recreative, destructive and contradictory nature of the motivating centre, the womb of war—I try to make that momentary peace which is a poem. . . . a poem of mine is, or should be, a watertight section of the stream that is flowing all ways, all warring images in it should be reconciled for that small stop of time."[12]

II

The same mysticism appears in the short stories that Thomas wrote up to 1939, during the period of his early poetic style.

The visions of "An Adventure from a Work in Progress," "A Prospect of the Sea," and the strange map in "The Map of Love" are fuller descriptions of the ultimate reality reported by the poems; sometimes, as we shall see, they make use of the same language and imagery. These stories contain a considerable admixture of themes from Welsh folklore, and it is possible, in view of their relationship with the poems, that Thomas' mythic consciousness has its roots in the folklore of the region where he was born, lived most of his life, and did most of his work. But whatever the source of his mysticism may have been, it must be emphasized that Thomas arrived at it through his own resources. The notebooks containing his early poems and drafts in the Lockwood Memorial Library at the University of Buffalo show Thomas seeking explanations for whatever was painful and unsatisfactory in his experience in the metaphysics of mysticism. Oppressed by loneliness, by the nightmare of industrial civilization, and by the apparent futility of life, he turned to the logic of the spirit.

There is, to be sure, considerable conventional nature-mysticism in these early drafts. Thomas feels that his loneliness can be relieved by the friendship of the snail and the tree, by the message of the bird's wing. But a series of four superior poems, written in May and June, 1933, when he was approaching his nineteenth birthday, record genuine spiritual conflicts and describe their resolution in the irrational, paradoxical language of mysticism.[13]

Several earlier poems anticipate the significant series of four. In "Twenty One," dated April 1, 1933, for example, Thomas complains of the fear he experiences in the dark and laments that there must be times when neither the sun nor the moon is visible. The solution to this difficulty is not to pray for perpetual daylight, but to find within himself a spiritual illumination superior to the sources of mortal light. The mystic elements in this poem include the conception of "light" as a continuous, undifferentiated principle, without regard to its source, and, most impressive, the decision, proposed by the last line, to seek relief in the spiritual discipline of recognizing the unity of opposites by perceiving that the night also sheds light. "Twenty Six," a long autobiographical narrative, after describing the chaos of experience with considerable realistic detail, compares it to the discords produced by a musician who does not know his keyboard. The resolution lies in learning to achieve a unity of time.

But we come then to a statement of mature mysticism that offers a coherent cosmic view instead of a mere escape from unsatisfactory conditions, in three poems written in May and June, 1933, and appearing in consecutive order in the February, 1933, notebook. The first of these, "Thirty One," has the elusive, ambiguous syntax characteristic of Thomas and a ritualistic incremental repetition sometimes found in his published verse. It defines the mystic state as being free of the senses and capable of accommodating various moral and physical paradoxes, including that of the unity of time; this condition is to be sharply distinguished, the poem insists, from commonplace religious attitudes. Further, all existence is a part of it, and future, past, and present and those who inhabit them are included in it. The final stanza undertakes to impress this fact upon the reader by a sudden intimate stroke, declaring that the activity of reading the poem is itself a manifestation of the greater existence.

In the following poem, "Thirty Two," dated May 20, 1933, Thomas identifies his own suffering with that of Jesus, and then moves on to the generalization that all things are identifiable with each other, that all of life is contained within each moment of it. Further, the all-including details of existence contain the contraries of life and death, pleasure and pain, so that they and the universe as a whole are dual in nature. This poem reflects three of the most familiar special conditions of mysticism. In seeing his own experiences as a counterpart of those of Jesus, Thomas eliminates the passage of time, conceiving of history as an unmoving, eternal moment. The consequent feeling that all things share a common identity is the mystic sense of the unity of being, and contradictions locked into every natural object set the stage for the drama of reconciliation which possesses the universe.

In "Thirty Three," dated May 23, 1933, Thomas charts a practical spiritual course to faith. It must begin with sympathy for the suffering that takes place in the universe, a recognition of the austere and terrifying facts of life. This should lead to an outraged skepticism and a rejection of God. But out of this burial must come a miraculous resurrection of belief strengthened by full knowledge of suffering and death. Having thus arrived at the mystical convictions that the universe as a whole is contained in each of its parts, that contraries share a common unity, and that true belief must be based on rejection, Thomas could say, in a poem called "Thirty Nine" written in July, 1933, that paradoxes lead to truth, and go on to declare that only a mystic reconciliation of life and death can produce ultimate truth. The role of the poet himself, he continues in "Thirty Nine," is to differentiate himself from others, to maintain detachment, and to court death in life.

III

For Thomas, conventional language is little more than a point of departure, a plastic medium to be shaped into unprecedented forms of expression. He once wrote, in answer to a question about his methods of composition:

I am a painstaking, conscientious, involved and devious craftsman in words, however unsuccessful the result so often appears, and to whatever wrong uses I may apply my technical paraphernalia. I use everything and anything to make my poems work and move in the direction I want them to: old tricks, new tricks, puns, portmanteau-words, paradox, allusion, paronomasia, paragram, catachresis, slang, assonantal rhymes, vowel rhymes, sprung rhythm. Every device there is in language is there to be used if you will.[14]

Language, as Thomas exploits its "twistings and convolutions," is turned at angles that will reflect the peculiar conditions and relationships of the timeless universe; the effect is to jar the reader out of his normal understanding of words. His rhetorical innovations observe neither limits nor consistency and are capable of moving from witty and tightly organized word play to the sort of loose and arbitrary associations characteristic of the most primitive uses of language. "All-hollowed man," "You with a bad coin in your socket," "Five sovereign fingers taxed the breath," and "chaste and the chaser" illustrate the sometimes outrageous style of his puns. Although he invents nonce words, as when he says that the Creator "shaped my clay-fellow," he prefers to exploit the resources prepared in advance by the accidents of language. Homonyms like "shell," "spade," "vice," and "rub" are often fitted into contexts which take advantage of their multiple meanings. Sometimes such words provide a point of connection between different areas of thought and, it may be supposed, acted in Thomas' mind as suggestions determining the development of his ideas or imagery. In the fifth poem of the "Altarwise by owl-light" sequence, for example, in which the angel Gabriel figures in the incongruous disguise of a cardsharp, the punning expression "trumped up," alluding both to the angel and the card game, but having a meaning separate from both, appears. At the end of "Before I knocked," Jesus says that his birth was both a blessing and an infliction by saying that God, in bringing him to birth, "doublecrossed my mother's womb." It is characteristic of Thomas to exploit the oddity that a slang phrase for deceit should involve the Christian symbol. Like Joyce, who had a photograph of the city of Cork framed in cork, he enjoyed the coincidences of language and regarded them as clues to an arcane system of relationships underlying immediate reality.

Thomas is reported to have kept a notebook he called a "dictionary," which was apparently a listing of words that offered rhetorical opportunities of this kind. The multiple meanings he attached to words are so private that, in the absence of his own glossary, they can be worked out only through careful examination of the various contexts in which they appear. "Weathers," as Thomas uses it, can mean the seasons of the year, the heavens, winds, or, in the sense of seasons of the soul, emotions. "Ride" is related to fertility, and often expresses movements of growth or energy as in "the riding Thames" and in "the green blooms ride upward."

Since opposites meet in Thomas' cosmos, a single word is sometimes used in antithetical senses. The point that words encompassing contradictory meanings are an archaic feature of language was made by Freud in his essay, "The Antithetical Sense of Primal Words," and Thomas' use of them suggests a primitive form of thought. Often there is a clue to these reversals, as in "last shocked beginning," but sometimes the word stands alone, forming an enigma. In "let us summon/Death from a summer woman" from the poem "I see the boys of summer," "death," as Tindall abruptly asserts in his explication of the poem, really means "birth." The grammatical phenomenon known as transference, the use of a word as another part of speech, is common in poetry generally; but Thomas is capable of carrying it very far, as in his use of "marrow" as a verb; in "Our eunuch dreams," where the noun appears adjectivally; and in "Jacob to the stars," where the proper name satisfies the context only if it is construed as a verb in the past tense. Ingenious and jocose neologisms occasionally appear: Jesus, regarded intimately and affectionately, is "my jack of Christ," and the body that burdens the spirit is "happy Cadaver."

Thomas' deliberate derangement of conventional language to suit the requirements of his private vision is well illustrated in the second line of "Button your bodice on a hump of splinters,/ My camel's eye will needle through the shrowd" [sic]. If the first line is interpreted as describing a gesture of disbelief, the second means that the speaker, God, or Jesus, will reach the skeptic in spite of himself. But it is also saying, in effect, "I know the original image of the needle's eye warned of the difficulty of reaching heaven. But just as I am discontent with that doctrine, I am discontent with the image expressing it, and I have reversed the image in order to controvert the doctrine. The eye now belongs to the camel, it is alive and can see clearly, and the needle is a symbol of mercy not obstruction, for it penetrates the deathlike garment of disbelief." It would not be wrong to sense in the disruption and reformation of conventional language found in Thomas' poetry a protest against the unimaginative view of reality reflected in ordinary language. "In thought and words," said Vernon Watkins of Thomas, "he was anarchic, challenging, with the certainty of that instinct which knows its own freshly discovered truth."[15]

Though Thomas' choice of words may sometimes seem arbitrary, his strangest locutions can usually be shown to be parts of a well-considered rhetorical fabric. The "whinnying light" of "How shall my animal" fits into a system of metaphors involving animals, including horses; the equally enigmatic "designed snow" from "In Country Sleep" is one of a number of allusions playing upon the fact that snowflakes have intricate symmetrical patterns. "Ferned and foxy woods" in "After the Funeral" means more than woods full of ferns and foxes; it echoes the "stuffed fox" and "stale fern" of Ann Jones's parlor, upon which the reversal of the poem as a whole pivots. On the other hand, a reference to the drowning of Susannah in "the bearded stream" in "Ballad of the Long-Legged Bait" seems to combine pointlessly the stream and the elders. Such arbitrary associations, more characteristic of the later than the earlier poems, may not be as haphazard as they seem, but they lack the acuity of Thomas' best poetic logic.

Notions of linguistic decorum have no place in Thomas' use of language. He is particularly indifferent to violations of what have been called "levels of usage." Such slang terms as "hophead" and "come a cropper" and an occasional Americanism like "scrams" are freely admitted into contexts that are otherwise serious, if not positively bardic. On the other hand, special terms like "hyleg" and "parhelion" sometimes appear inappropriately where the prevailing tone is familiar and informal. Thomas' practice of using different levels of abstraction, different classes of words, and different principles of metaphor in the same context causes considerable difficulty. To think of a bell as a "pulled house" requires that "pulled" be regarded as literal, and "house" as metaphoric. Since the line, "The fingers will forget green thumbs" occurs in a poem having as its point the interchange of capacities among the senses, the notion that fingers can forget may be acceptable; but the trite "green thumbs," clearly intended to serve as a variant for "fingers," has a homely quality that contrasts discordantly with the elaborate synesthetic pretensions of the other image. The line "Time's coral saint and the salt grief drown a foul sepulchre" requires the reader not only to equate the abstract "grief" with the sea but also to move in the opposite direction by equating a comparatively specific "saint" with a generalized sea. "A million minds gave suck to such a bud/As forks my eye" similarly involves a rapid shuttling about among various levels of metaphor, the only certain one being the literal "eye."

John Bayley, in *The Romantic Survival,* has vividly described the difficulty the reader feels when he is confronted by this complex use of language:

It is only with great agility and understanding that the reader can accept such varying usages as each functional and necessary in its kind. . . . it is as if—to adopt a rough-and-ready metaphor—our progress through it was not a smooth expanding flow, but rather an obstacle race at different levels scrambling over objects, falling into holes, and clambering painfully out again to nerve ourselves for a jump across a chasm or a tightrope walk between two trees.[16]

But he adds that, in spite of the doubts this ordeal naturally arouses, the intricacies of Thomas' style are probably justified by his attempts to discover "the ways in which language can be brought more and more directly into contact with feelings and things."

IV

Most of Thomas' linguistic derangements are effected in the interests of imagery. Metaphor, analogy, and symbols—the principal expressive resources of mysticism—are fundamental and pervasive elements of his verse. The imagery of his early poems is probably unparalleled in its complexity and obscurity; the same metaphoric methods, and some of the same images persist in the later stages of his style but are considerably thinned out and thus rendered more accessible. The difficulties of Thomas' images, like those of his words, are a straining against the bounds of the intelligible, a result of his attempt to encompass the multiple identities, related opposites, and changing shapes that inhabit his vision of reality. Thomas' metaphoric method combines communicative power with inexplicitness. He seldom signals the presence of imagery by using the language of overt comparison. His metaphors are usually "submerged"; that is, only one term of the metaphoric comparison is actually mentioned, the other being left to inference. In "The force that through the green fuse drives the flower," for example, the "fuse," is, of course, the stem of the plant; but most of these suggested comparisons are, as we shall see, less obvious. In fact, the reader is often uncertain whether or not he is confronted with metaphoric language.

As Elder Olson has pointed out, it is often hard to tell whether Thomas intends a particular term literally or metaphorically.[17] In a line describing an episode of creation, "One bough of bone across the rooting air," it is impossible to tell whether the metaphor begins with "bough" or "bone." This merging of tenor and vehicle, one of the recurring features of Thomas' imagery, resembles a characteristic of language Cassirer has described as a consequence of the obsessive nature of mythic thought. In the mythic use of words, he says, "The potential between 'symbol' and 'meaning' is resolved; in place of a more or less adequate 'expression,' we find a relation of identity or complete congruence between 'image' and 'object,' between the name and the thing."[18]

Thomas, after introducing his metaphors unobtrusively, is capable of subjecting them to subtle and elaborate development. He is a great craftsman of the sustained metaphor; once having established a metaphoric relationship, he may pursue it energetically, drawing parallels and consequences out of the original comparison and transposing attributes from one term to another. A clear, if labored example is found in "Do you not father me." The speaker of the poem compares himself, in the basic metaphor, to a house on the seashore, "a lovers' house," where each member of the family plays a particular role. The opening question, "Do you not father me . . . cast in her stone?" is a reference, painfully literal, but logical within the metaphor, to parenthood; the father has shaped the child out of material supplied by the mother. In the first stanza, the speaker declares that he possesses a tower, turrets, and windows; but in the third stanza the direction of the metaphor is reversed momentarily as a tower speaks. In the third stanza, the speaker declares that, as a prelude to a kind of resurrection, he has been sacrificed; the destroyer, he says, making use of the house metaphor, "razed my wooden folly." Nevertheless, says the final stanza, his love will survive as a reproach to the guilty parents, "Woe to the windy masons . . . ." Further extensions appear in "tower death" and in the reference to God as "the towering tiler."

The difficulties created by the intensive development of single metaphors are compounded by Thomas' usual practice of weaving metaphors together. Christine Brooke-Rose, in her *Grammar of Metaphor,* has shown that this procedure involves a number of hazards, as in the case of genitive metaphors, those involving a syntax of possession:

The Genitive metaphor added to other metaphors runs into two dangers: in sustained allegory, the second metaphor is, strictly speaking not metaphoric in relation to the first, but only in relation to its proper term . . . so that the second metaphor often destroys the first, or, when the Genitive relationship is one of basic identity, the effect is of mere splitting up or tautology. Alternatively, the second metaphor can be metaphoric in relation to the first, in which case a new metaphor is added and runs the risk of being "mixed."[19]

She points out that in Thomas' lines, "Where no wax is, the candle shows its hairs," if the candle is a metaphoric equivalent for the phallus, "hairs" must be metaphoric with regard to the candle but not with regard to the original term. In her example, "My fathers' globe knocks on its nave and sings," the second metaphor, "nave," simply contributes to the obscurity, for since the "fathers" are not clearly identified, their "globe" and the "nave" are increasingly indefinite. Miss Brooke-Rose does not imply that linked metaphors are inherently unsatisfactory, but her observations that they may generate vagueness, contradictions, and fragmentation are clearly relevant to Thomas' style.

Thomas' way of extending and linking his metaphors is a further indication of the kinship between his rhetoric and the functioning of the primitive imagination. His imagery seems to be the product of a process like the "fusion" Frederick Clarke Prescott has described as characteristic of mythic thought.

Sun and *man* were fancied alike . . . and so were combined into a *Sun God.* It was a little like putting one photograph on top of another to make a composite. Since it was not, however, a matter of mere putting together or mechanical combination, it would be better to say that the two fused or grew vitally into one, thus forming a new creature. This god of the sun was alive . . . he was accordingly ranked with other existent persons, and was in turn susceptible of further combination. Thus a tree might be fused with a woman, or clouds with sheep, or swords with serpents; and . . . this new creature in turn might be fused with any primary element or with any other secondary one—that is, the goddess might turn into a cloud or a bird, or into another goddess. Since each fusion depended merely upon some caprice of association . . . the number of such combinations was endless. . . . The devious paths of this maze can never be retraced.[20]

We are warned, therefore, that rational analysis cannot satisfactorily explain Thomas' images. They obviously do not imitate life or follow logical relations, and their interest does not arise from the fact that they may correspond with spiritual platitudes. In Thomas' story, "The Orchards," the poet, who bears Thomas' middle name, Marlais, concludes that "the word is too much with us"; and, as the scene before him seems to be transformed into visible metaphors, he cries "Image, all image." The episode suggests Thomas' way of thinking of imagery: not as an expressive device, but as a vessel of ultimate experience, a self-sufficient, imaginative construction made up of raw material found through the senses. Thomas' use of imagery is based upon many (though not all) of the presuppositions effectively expounded in Frank Kermode's *The Romantic Image*. The significance of Thomas' metaphors is inseparably embodied in themselves, so that—to use the figure Kermode has adapted from Yeats—it is impossible to tell the dancer from the dance. They are meaningful, not arbitrary; but they are organized intuitively rather than intellectually. They are intended, not to represent something already known, but to act as revelations of something unknown or known only subconsciously. The truths of Thomas' images are not those of ordinary experience, but those of his mysticism, which the images themselves convey. They are validated, not by reference to experience, but by imaginative acceptance.

Though it is isolated from ordinary experience, this imagery has its own environment, a self-created, imaginative realm which it serves to illustrate and epitomize. The repetitiveness so often observed in Thomas' verse brings us to the major fact that many of his images belong to a fairly consistent and continuous body of metaphor. Thomas seems to have had fixed in his mind a few metaphoric relationships to which he reverted, in poem after poem, for imagery. This results not only in repetition but also in the development of whole families of metaphor from central cores through loose and freely-imagined associations, as well as through linguistic ambiguities. These key metaphors resemble what Mark Schorer, speaking of fiction, has called a "matrix of analogy," a correspondence between two terms that serves as a source of further correspondences as the implications of the relationship are developed.

Images derived from these central metaphors are so common in *18 Poems* that the volume almost seems to be unified into a single text by its preoccupation with a handful of rhetorical figures. We find these key metaphors used less frequently as Thomas' style changed, but the vocabulary associated with them persists in his later verse. Replying to Henry Treece's objections that his early poems were diffuse and that they seemed to belong to a larger whole, Thomas admitted that they shared a continuity of metaphor. In them, he said, ". . . images were left dangling over the formal limits, and dragged the poem into another. . . ."[21] This means not only that their common fund of metaphor brings many of the poems into close relationships with one another but that the point of a particular image may not be clarified within an individual poem. The reader is forced to consider it in terms of other places where it appears, so that its proper context is Thomas' poetry as a whole; and the short stories written before 1938 must be included, for the key metaphors appear prominently in them.

Thomas described his method of devising imagery in a statement that has become very well known. In his letter to Henry Treece he wrote:

I make one image—though "make" is not the word; I let, perhaps an image be "made" emotionally in me and then apply to it what intellectual and critical forces I possess—let it breed another, let that image contradict the first, make of the third image bred out of the other two together, a fourth contradictory image, and let them all, within my imposed formal limits, conflict. Each image holds within it the seed of its own destruction, and my dialectal method, as I understand it, is a constant building up and breaking down of the images that come out of the central seed, which is itself destructive and constructive at the same time.[22]

He begins then with an image which arises in his mind spontaneously; this passive beginning explains why so many of his metaphors have common origins in a few favorite key images established in his thoughts "emotionally." The "intellectual" and "critical" treatment is no doubt the ingenious elaboration the image then undergoes. By saying that "each image holds within itself the seed of its own destruction," Thomas appears to mean that it embodies what Ernst Kris has called a disjunctive ambiguity; that is, it has two meanings opposed to one another.[23] For example, the recurrent comparison of life to a disease can take the form of either "wintry fever," or "love's first fever." That is, it can refer to a pathological state leading to death or to the fervent emotions that lead to procreation and the renewal of life. As Thomas said elsewhere in his letter to Treece, the images are "warring images" from a "warring stream" of thought. They reflect the dialectic pattern of Thomas' vision of nature by bringing irreconcilables together, or by lending themselves to contradictory interpretations as in "the fathering worm" and in "the dark brides, the widows of the night." The "building up" and "breaking down" Thomas mentions would then be the exploitation of the image in opposing directions.

Familiarity with these recurring images is indispensable to the understanding of Thomas' poems. I should like to begin with one which illustrates both the dialectic quality and the flexibility of these metaphoric structures. As early as "Where once the waters of your face" in *18 Poems* we meet a "green unraveller,/ His scissors oiled. . . ." This is the first appearance of a figure often encountered in the poems, the bearer of a sharp, bright cutting instrument who is sometimes a representative of life, as a midwife cutting the umbilical cord would be, and sometimes an Atropos-like agent of death or destruction. Perhaps this metaphor originates in Welsh folklore, for we are told in the short story "The School for Witches" that "A vampire with a scissors was a Pembroke devil." A devil bearing scissors and named "Domdaniel" appears as a figure threatening castration in an unpublished poem Thomas wrote in 1933.[24]

This personification is the "central seed," dialectic in nature; for, as Thomas puts it in his explanation, it is capable of being built up and broken down into conflicting images of birth or destruction. In "I, in my intricate image," this figure is a surgeon, and the operation performed is an "antiseptic funeral." In "When, like a running grave" Domdaniel undergoes the transformation of "Comes, like a scissors stalking, tailor age," and the blade-bearing tailor reappears in "Twenty-four years," where he brilliantly symbolizes the continuity of birth and death by squatting in "the natural doorway" like both a fetus and a tailor, "sewing a shroud for a journey." The figure of the tailor as the arbiter of life and death is developed into new metaphoric forms in "Once below a time." There, since the tailors are deities, the body they create is a suit of clothes, "my pinned-around-the spirit/Cut-to-measure flesh." And the poet complains both that their creation is slop work and that the tailors are poor workmen, "the famous stitch droppers." The master tailor sews "with nerves for cotton," and Thomas describes himself as a "boy of common thread." We understand what Thomas meant by saying that he left images dangling when we encounter such enigmatic phrases as "sewing tides" in "How soon the servant sun" and "bridal blade" in "All all and all," for they are explicable only in terms of this whole complex of imagery.

One of the most pervasive of these key associations is the identification of the human body with the earth. The notion that the body is a microcosm of the universe, and the reverse equivalence, the attribution of human capacities to nature through the pathetic fallacy are, of course, among the most familiar properties of Romantic poetry. But Thomas manipulates the metaphor and its consequences in ways that renew and deepen their significance. He bases the relationship upon the fact that man springs from and returns to the earth, so that the two share a physical existence. There are bones in the hills; and, when the dead child in "A Refusal to Mourn" is buried, she will join those who have died before her and have been dissolved into "the grains beyond age." But it follows that the earth shares also man's spiritual and sentient capacities; in this strange realm the soil squeals and the boulders bleed.

The body-earth identification is the subject of at least two of Thomas' early poems: "The force that through the green fuse," and "Light breaks where no sun shines." The image appears in its most explicit form, perhaps, in "Ears in the turrets hear," where the self is

　　　　tnu ⍺land bound
　　　By a thin sea of flesh
　　　And a bone coast. . . .

Its usual appearances, however, are far less obvious. It is covertly involved, for example, in "A process in the weather of the heart," whose imagery is constructed on the idea that man experiences the same conflict of opposing forces found in the universe at large. Damp and dry, night and day, birth and death—all are parts of "a process" equally dominant over man and nature; it is described in terms drawn alternately from allusions to the body and the earth, so that the two merge together, and all the references become metaphoric. The changing conditions of the heart and veins are therefore "weather," analogous to the changing conditions of nature. This association leads in turn to "weather winds that blow not down the bone" and to "the twelve-winded marrow" in "Foster the light," as though energies deep in the tissues of the body were not to be distinguished from those of external nature.

This key metaphor is brilliantly exploited in the second and third stanzas of "I, in my intricate image." There, the "unravelling" of the fabric of nature by the processes of spring produces material from which man is raised. The other self the poet creates with this material retains the marks of his nonhuman origin and emerges as "my man of leaves and the bronze root." The same logic produces such imagery as "ancient woods of my blood" in "On no work of words" and "throats where many rivers meet" from "In the white giant's thigh." In "How shall my animal," Thomas tells the hostile beast of his inner self that he has subdued it: he has "dug your grave in my breast." Since the earth serves as a grave, the body, which is another earth, can do so too. This aspect of the body-earth metaphor seems responsible for the idea that the body, like the earth, is tunneled through with worms. Hence, in "All all and all," Thomas addresses the flesh as "Worm in the scalp, the staked and fallow," attributing to it three properties of earth: it harbors worms, it can be penetrated with a stake (an allusion to vampires), and it has its times of infertility.

Since existence, in Thomas' Heraclitean view of it, is a conflict, an apposite, if trite metaphoric equivalent for it is offered by actual warfare. But Thomas' way of developing this dangerously stale image produces strikingly original results. In "The seed-at-zero," the conjunction of sperm and womb is described as an attack on a besieged town, a metaphor which is elaborated throughout the poem, imposing its own order on everything until it achieves the quality of a systematic delusion, as if it were a paranoiac symptom. The two areas of the metaphor are merged, as they are in the refrain describing coition: "Dumbly and divinely stumbling/Over the manwaging line." and "Dumbly and divinely leaping/Over the warbearing line." Not only physical love, but the whole world of nature and spirit is transformed into a battle scene, as in "Through the rampart of the sky/Shall the star-flanked seed be riddled. . . ."

An interesting specialization of the battle metaphor occurs when spiritual events are expressed in imagery based specifically on the trench warfare of World War I. In "Reminiscences of Childhood" Thomas has told how talk of the war made a vague but profound impression on him. It seems as if this stratum of his imagination, enriched, no doubt, by impressions drawn from movies, supplies the imagery for the second part of "My world is pyramid," where a battle scene appears as a counterpart of the Passion:

> I hear, through dead men's drums, the riddled lads,
> Strewing their bowels from a hill of bones,
> Cry Eloi to the guns.

The same associations control the metaphor used to describe the second death in "I dreamed my genesis" as one caused by shrapnel and gas. They are also lurking in the complicated fourth stanza of "Before I knocked" in the lines "And flesh was snipped to cross the lines/Of gallow crosses on the liver. . . ." These lines are about birth, and Christ is saying that the passage from pre-existence into actual life was as hazardous as crossing the lines of barbed wire on a battlefield.

The movies are also responsible, no doubt, for Thomas' allusions to vampires and to the legends concerning them. In a macabre unpublished poem, the dead, including vampires, are described as friends of the living. The vampire is mentioned in "My world is pyramid," but most of the allusions elsewhere occur in the form of fleeting verbal references. In the vampire myth, sucking is, of course, a way of taking life, as well as nourishment; and a stake is driven through the heart of the preying corpse to immobilize it. These are favorite words with Thomas, and often appear to allude to vampires.

One of Thomas' most impressive key metaphors compares the general phenomenon of life to an explosion whose force originated at the moment of creation and spread steadily through the universe. This burst of universal energy has its beneficent aspects in the form of growth and fertility, its negative ones in the form of destruction and death. The creator who speaks in "When once the twilight locks no longer" states that he has endowed man with divine energy, "My fuses timed to charge his heart/ He blew like powder to the light. . . ." The force that drives the flower through the *fuse* of its stem in Thomas' best-known poem must be explosive, and it also *blasts* the tree roots. The metaphor is used in the poem "In the beginning" where man appears when "Blood shot and scattered to the winds of light/The ribbed original of love." The "rotating shell" of "I dreamed my genesis" and the "trigger and scythe" of "All all and all" are among the images in this complex. Although Thomas had a fund of favorite words for vigorous activities, including "bounce," "spin," "lunge," and "ride," the explosion imagery appears when he reaches for a means of expressing some ultimate action. As late as "Over Sir John's hill," the predatory "hawk on fire" has a "viperish fuse," and the image assumes spiritual values in "the judge blown bedlam" of "Vision and Prayer," where the explosion raises a cloud of holy dust.

It is odd that a poet who is both a Romantic and a mystic should make use of the eighteenth-century analogy between nature and the machine, but this identification is one of Thomas' most fruitful key images. In describing organic processes as if they were mechanical actions, in identifying living things or organs with machines, in using oil to represent living energy, and in referring to the spiritual power that animates the universe as the sort of power used by machinery, Thomas is certainly extrapolating from the notion that the universe is a mechanism. No doubt the metaphor implies a wry criticism of the mechanization of modern life, for it occurs in an unpublished early poem in which Thomas complains of industrial civilization.[25]

In "The Mouse and the Woman," an early short story, the woman of whom the hero is dreaming thinks in her delirium of "the levers of the trees and the toothed twigs," a vision which gives biological energies mechanical forms. In "My hero bares his nerves," the nervous system is a circuit of electrical wires attached to the skull, the source of its power. An image from Part I of "Our eunuch dreams" also identifies mental with mechanical energy by saying that the material of dreams is raised "by midnight pulleys." This identification, like the others, is elaborated in fanciful ways. The comparison of the earth to a car, as well as the association of oil and living energy, seem present in the lines from "In the beginning" where life "pumped from the earth and rock/The secret oils that drive the grass."

The fact that machines are made of metal is the source of a considerable family of metaphors identifying metal with human flesh. "All all and all the dry worlds lever" has "the heart in the ribbing metal," and "stroke of mechanical flesh"; "I in my intricate image" speaks of the "bronze root" of man and brings together the notions that man is essentially a spirit clad in flesh and that his origin is the sea, in the lines "My ghost in his metal neptune/Forged in man's mineral."

Much of Thomas' imagery, particularly, but not exclusively that in *18 Poems* and *Twenty-five Poems,* is developed in this way, through arbitrary elaborations of the kind described by Prescott, arriving at nearly unintelligible metaphoric conclusions from a fairly conventional point of origin. For example the metaphoric identification of wax and flesh has as its consequences the phallic candle and the idea that the body consumes itself with the fire of life. Since love, fertility, and the warmth of the body are thought of as a disease, a "wintry fever" that eventually kills, they are described as "contagious." Blood is associated with words and knowledge, so that the heart is "spelling in the scurry/Of chemic blood," and "wordy wounds are printed."

It will be noticed that Thomas elaborates his metaphors by moving on the concrete level. In a conventional metaphor, the similarity binding the two terms together is ordinarily abstract or general. Matthew Arnold, hearing the surf at Dover Beach, reported that ". . . we/Find also in the sound a thought," and he turned to the abstract notion of retreat equally applicable to the religion of his day and the sea to arrive at the image of "the Sea of Faith." Thomas, however, develops his metaphors, not by falling back on a vague general quality, but by multiplying specific resemblances and passing attributes from one term of the metaphor to the other. The implications to be drawn from the body-earth metaphor are not that the body has endurance or immortality, but that it has roots, winds, worms, and so on.

This process is illustrated by the delirium of the dying poet in the short story, "The Visitor": "It pleased him to look upon the unmoving waves of the bedclothes, and think himself an island set somewhere in the south sea. Upon this island of rich and miraculous plants, the seeds grown fruits hung from the trees and, smaller than apples, dropped with the pacific winds on to the ground to lie there and be the harbourers of the summer slugs."[26] This treatment of metaphor assumes that meaning is not something separable from physical reality but inherent in it. "Thomas," observes John Bayley in *The Romantic Survival*, "is haunted by the indivisibility of mind and matter."[27] As the key image involving language and nature declares, he considers matter itself articulate. This rhetorical practice is another point of correspondence with the primitive, mythmaking imagination in which, according to Cassirer,

. . . thought does not dispose freely over the data of intuition, in order to relate and compare them to each other, but is captivated and enthralled by the intuition which suddenly confronts it. It comes to rest in the immediate experience. . . . Instead of a widening of intuitive experience, we find here its extreme limitation; instead of expansion that would lead through greater and greater spheres of being, we have here an impulse toward concentration; instead of extensive distribution, intensive compression. This focusing of all forces on a single point is the prerequisite for all mythical thinking and mythical formulation.[28]

Generalization is foreign to this mode of thought. Only literalness and immediacy are intelligible within it. Thomas, we recall, insisted that his poetry should be taken literally. In his objection

to Edith Sitwell's reading of an image from the first section of
"Altarwise by owl-light," he said that the way to read the image
was to linger on all its concrete and sensuous implications: "She
doesn't take the literal meaning: that a world-devouring ghost
creature bit the horror of to-morrow from a gentleman's loins.
'A jaw for news' . . . means that the mouth of the creature can
taste already the horror that has not yet come; or can sense its
coming, can thrust its tongue into news that has not yet been
made, can savour the enormity of the progeny before the seed
stirs. . . ."[29] He develops his metaphors, not by dwelling on
abstract relations, but by intensifying and enriching their actuality. As Cassirer says of mythic conceptions, "Here is no 'reference' and 'meaning'; every content of consciousness to which
the mind is directed is immediately translated into terms of
actual presence and effectiveness. Here thought does not confront
its data in an attitude of free contemplation . . . but is simply
captivated by a total impression."[30]

The preoccupation with a limited area of metaphor which has
led some critics to observe that Thomas' constant reversion to
particular notions, images, and words has an obsessive quality,
also has its counterpart in mythic thought. Thomas extends the
parallels between the two terms of his metaphor until they seem
irrational; the logic of the image takes control. Reason and actuality do not disappear, but they give way before the momentum of imagination, assuming new shapes. This is shown by
Thomas' explanation of two lines from "I make this in a warring
absence": "A calm wind blows that raised the trees like hair/
Once where the soft snow's blood was turned to ice." In the
interests of expressing the terrifying power of his wind, Thomas
has supplied his snowflakes with circulatory systems. He explained, ". . . a wind had blown that had frightened everything &
created the first ice & the first frost by frightening the falling
snow so much that the blood of each flake froze."[31]

This derangement of ordinary perception is another effect of
the mythmaking consciousness described by Cassirer: "All other
things are lost to a mind thus enthralled; all bridges between the
concrete datum and the systematized totality of experience are
broken; only the present reality, a mythic or linguistic conception stresses and shapes it, fills the entire subjective realm. So

this one content of experience must reign over practically the whole experiential world."[32]

This dominance of Thomas' metaphoric associations is rarely developed fully within a single poem. Instead, as we have seen, their effects turn up in the form of images and epithets repeated in scattered poems and stories. Further, the suggestion often arises that even the separate images are related to each other and form continuous fields of metaphor. The motif of the explosion of fertility and that of the battlefield of nature seem allied to each other. The notion of inner winds and weathers seems to be a consequence of the body-earth metaphor. The machine image seems responsible for the terminology of metals and minerals often applied to the body. We have noted that individual terms, such as "forks," which means both the devil's pitchfork and the branching of a plant, and "sucks," which applies both to the vampire and to the suckling infant, effect similar farfetched connections. Perhaps these correspondences arise simply because the different figures of speech are accommodated to each other within individual poems. But when they lean together in this way, Thomas' images assume the appearance of fragments from a network of private symbols resembling the systems of Blake and Yeats. They seem to be brief, enigmatic glimpses of an arcane iconography embodying a lost world of incommunicable cosmic thoughts. They certainly support the impression that the poems in which they occur have a subliminal continuity with each other. "I agree," wrote Thomas, "that each of my earlier poems might appear to constitute a section from one long poem; that is because I was not successful in making a momentary peace with my images at the correct moment . . . the warring stream ran on over the insecure barriers. . . ."[33]

V

The exceptionally well-developed formal and sensuous qualities of Thomas' poetry seem to be a consequence of his feeling that language has a reality equal to that of material things. This strong sense of the objective reality of his work is suggested by Vernon Watkins' report that Thomas wrote the manuscript of one of his stories on a large piece of cardboard so that he could see the whole thing at once, as if it were an object. The complicated structures of contrast, balance, repetition, parallelism, and the thick texture of sound effects give his poems the palpable, resistant solidity of something material. Thomas is the most resourceful of craftsmen in the phonic qualities of poetry; he is approached in this regard only by Hopkins, who is far less subtle. He uses the whole range of possibilities offered by the sound of language to knit his poems together into tightly unified forms. There are hardly two consecutive lines anywhere in Thomas' poems that do not manifest active craftsmanship of this kind, though it may appear in subtle forms.

Thomas is an unparalleled master of versification and metric form; his virtuosity shows itself not merely in his power to control rhythms and verse patterns but also in his ability to invent and manipulate new and interesting forms. He has gone further than any earlier poet in substituting assonance and consonant-rhyme for actual rhyme, accepting almost any correspondence of sound as a structural element. This characteristic, combined with his preference for the feminine ending, does much to give his early verse its admirable muted quality. Clear shifts and developments are perceptible in his practice. While he seems concerned in *18 Poems* primarily with the sort of discipline which packs elaborate metaphorical arguments into tight and unvarying stanzas like those of "All all and all" or "Our eunuch dreams," his later poems aim at elaborate virtuoso effects. The extreme baroque convolutions of the stanza of "Over Sir John's hill" and the lush, ringing music of "In Country Sleep" and "Fern Hill" display a very different use of poetic sound.

While the other aspects of his style changed, Thomas never dropped his method of organizing his verse according to syllables rather than the conventional metrical feet. Ralph Maud's studies and observations of manuscripts show that Thomas sought, and usually achieved, absolute regularity in the number of syllables he put into a line.[34] The regularity of his lines and stanza forms is a matter of syllables, and the effect is created by the containment of very free metrical variations within nearly unvarying syllable counts. The stanza of "My hero bares his nerves," for example, has lines of ten, seven, ten, seven and eight syllables, with no real irregularities. In some of his later poems, where Thomas exercises his metrical ingenuity fully, as in "Vision and Prayer" and "Over Sir John's hill," the length of lines can vary between one and fifteen syllables; but the variations are strictly duplicated, with very little irregularity, in each stanza.

Thomas' syntax and word patterns are used not only for the traditional function of expressing meaning but also as elements of poetic structure. Inversion, repetition, parallelism, significant variation, appositions, series consisting of contrasting members, and ellipses producing significant juxtapositions are all parts of his repertoire. The poem that begins "The hand that signed the paper felled a city" makes its point that the action was virulent and had lasting effects by the variant, "The hand that signed the treaty bred a fever." Similarly, the reversal of meaning in "Today, this insect" is represented by the contrast between "The insect certain is the plague of fables" and the significant variant, "The insect fable is the certain promise." In the lines

> Incarnate devil in a talking snake,
> The central plains of Asia in his garden,
> In shaping-time the circle stung awake. . . .

"circle" is the misplaced object of "stung," which is divided from its subject "devil" by the reversed second line, whose meaning is, "In his garden, in the central plains of Asia."

As every reader of Thomas can testify, his venturesome explorations in quest of structural devices of this kind cause much difficulty and obscurity, and Thomas seems unwilling to use the conventions of punctuation to relieve moments of confusion. For example,

> There the dark blade and wanton sighing her down
> To a haycock couch and the scythes of his arms
> Rode and whistled a hundred times. . . .

contains a parenthetical participial modifier that should be set off by commas, but Thomas seems to intend the temporary ambiguity presented by the juxtaposition of "wanton sighing." In these lines from "How shall my animal:" "Sigh long, clay cold, lie shorn,/Cast high, stunned on gilled stone. . . ."—the five groups of words separated by the commas sound parallel, but soon emerge as two imperatives divided from each other and followed by adjectives modifying what they are addressing. The following lines from "A grief ago" do not yield to analysis at all:

> Who is my grief. . . .
> Was who was folded on the rod the aaron
> Rose cast to plague,
> The horn and ball of water on the frog
> Housed in the side.

At least part of the difficulty here seems due to syntax or word order, though the fact that a single line contains three words that might be either noun or verb—"Rose cast to plague," and the odd use of "aaron" as a common noun are in themselves obstacles to clarity. This is an extreme example of the way in which Thomas' use of syntax as a poetic element may conflict with its usual function: that of forming a coherent pattern of meaning.[35]

CHAPTER 3

18 Poems

I

18 Poems was not written as a unit. Thomas assembled the volume simply by choosing the best poems he had written up to the time of its publication. But in admitting to Treece that each of his early poems was like a passage from a longer work, he might have added that they appear to be from the same work, for they have in common the primitive thought processes and the fund of private metaphoric associations described in Chapter 2. Moreover, many of them undertake, either explicitly or by implication, the same theme: the way in which the dialectic of life and death manifested in the material world finds its resolution in the absolute vision available to mysticism. Though each of the poems would yield a total statement of this mysticism if the implications of its rhetoric were extended, no one of them has Thomas' metaphysics in general as its subject. In saying that each of his poems was "a watertight section of the stream that is flowing all ways, all warring images within it should be reconciled for that small stop of time,"[1] Thomas seems to have meant that they move through a larger medium of ideas, temporarily organizing, without assimilating them. It is therefore difficult to fix upon any one subject as the theme of any one of the *18 Poems*. Nevertheless, a grouping by themes is convenient for purposes of discussion, and can be useful if we remember that while each poem may emphasize a particular point, it alludes, through its rhetoric, to Thomas' whole vision.

The piece in Thomas' first volume that most closely approaches the status of a definitive statement of the whole of man's experience is "A process in the weather of the heart." "Process," said David Aivaz, ". . .is the basic theme of all Thomas' poems," and he adds that it is the absolute reality with which individual beings must be reconciled.[2] In this poem, a series of paradoxes expressed in insistent stanzaic and syntactic parallelisms asserts the duality of the process of change to which the individual human being and his counterpart, the universe, are subjected. On the one hand, "A process in the eye forewarns/The bones of blindness," and, on the other, "A darkness in the weather of the eye/Is half its light." In a world of simultaneous time, "the quick and dead" are indistinguishable from each other; and, since both are temporary forms of constantly changing matter, they are "two ghosts."

The first four stanzas illustrate the tendency of Thomas' poems to imitate timelessness by circling repetitively about their centers, but the final stanza moves on to an expansion of meaning. The subject of the first part of the poem is the body; but "weather," "quarter of the veins," "fathomed sea" and "unangled land" broach a submerged metaphoric term which is suddenly made literal as the last stanza begins, "A process in the weather of the world. . . ." Thus, the force that "turns ghost to ghost, "or produces the alternation of spirit and matter, is a universal one. The poem closes as the "process" "Pulls down the shabby curtains of the skin;/And the heart gives up its dead." These apparently pessimistic images are also promises of renewal that maintain the balanced statement of the poem.

The reiterative structure of "A process in the weather of the heart" presents existence in the form of a single ambivalent entity, as it appears to the mystic; but "I dreamed my genesis" sees it with mortal eyes, as a sequence. The dreamer, who speaks for mankind in general, experiences births and deaths as a succession of events. But the terms he uses attest to their ultimate identity with each other, as in "I dreamed my genesis and died again," and birth is

> second
> Rise of the skeleton and
> Rerobing of the naked ghost.

Thomas' images of the battlefield and the machine collaborate with each other through the first three stanzas. The metaphor of the explosion of fertility appears in the speaker's statement that he came to birth, in the conflict of nature, "breaking/Through the rotating shell." Using the vocabulary of the machine image, he says his birth was a "journey/In bottom gear through night-geared man," as though human beings were motor-driven machines, and the states of sleeping and waking were different gears.

A more felicitous result of Thomas' literal-minded insistence on the details of his metaphors is "marching heart," where the heart's beating is, on the whole, smoothly transferred to the requirements of the war analogy. The battlefield scene in stanza five is Thomas' metaphor for the stage in the cycle of nature where death is put to the uses of life; the body of the dead soldier mingles with and fertilizes the soil, so that "Manhood/Spat up from the resuffered pain." In the final stanza, this material rebirth is translated into spiritual terms; after passing through the sea, "Adam's brine," a symbol of ancient evil, the speaker now turns to the light. He moves from his repetitive dream of mortal suffering to a vision of the renewal suggested, through a different kind of imagery, at the end of "A process in the weather of the heart."

18 Poems assumes a continuity between nature and the stories of Christ and Adam. "Before I knocked" has as its theme this interlocking of natural and spiritual worlds. This poem is one of the least problematic of the *18 Poems,* but it does compel the reader to confront the paradoxes and special conditions of Thomas' mysticism. The speaker of the poem, the unborn Jesus, begins by declaring his kinship with the processes and elements of nature. He then argues that, since he underwent mortal suffering before his birth, his experiences constitute an eternal reality and that he is a unique mingling of material and spiritual—a "mortal ghost."

The two leading assertions of the poem are contained in the lines, "As yet ungotten I did suffer," and "I who was rich was made the richer/By sipping at the vine of days." The first illustrates one of the obvious conditions of the poem, the simultaneity of time; the second formulates the event with which most of the poem is occupied: the coming of Christ, the entrance of an immortal being into the perplexities of the human condition. The paradoxes of Christ's speech are attempts to encompass the contradictions of his venture into the human dimension of time, where he knew existence as it appears to creatures who think of it as a passing sequence, a "vine of days." The last four lines remind us that this experience of mortality was also suffered by God, who inhabited Christ's body. The "doublecrossed" of the last line, as Tindall has observed, is "crowded" with meanings; it signifies not only the blessing and deception involved in the fate God chose for Christ but also His "crossing" back and forth into the current of human life.[3]

Though only a few of the images of the poem go beyond conventional limits, they interestingly illustrate a number of Thomas' private associations. The paradoxical "fathering worm" reflects Thomas' awareness that, within the cycle of nature, the dissolution of the body is also a preparation for new life. The fourth stanza contains two complex condensed images, thoroughly characteristic of Thomas' rhetoric. In "The rack of dreams my lily bones/Did twist into a living cipher," the brilliant invention of "lily bones" suggests that the bones of the embryonic Jesus are soft, delicate, and sacred like Easter lilies. The image describes the skeleton of the child as it would look before birth (under the X-ray, for example) as a tangled ideogram, a "living cipher." But it also has connotations relating to the development of thought; the dawning mental processes, twisted on the "rack" of primitive instincts and desires, become the mysterious "cipher" of the psyche. The last lines of the stanza make use of three separate scenes or episodes:

> And flesh was snipped to cross the lines
> Of gallow crosses on the liver
> And brambles in the wringing brains.

The subject here is God's entry into human form, and this event is described through two analogues: the Crucifixion, and the actions of a battlefield patrol. The three scenes are identified with each other through the device of shifting from one framework of allusion to another in the course of a single grammatical statement. In coming into the territory of mortality, God "crossed the lines"; he "snipped," not barbed wire, but the flesh of Jesus' body, through the Crucifixion. The battlefield where the crosses and brambles appear is Jesus' mortal form, insisted upon, with the merciless concrete literalism typical of Thomas' primitive rhetoric, through "liver" and "brains."

II

The idea that the natural world possesses the semantic properties of language is so prominent in Thomas' thought that it forms one of his key metaphors. This correspondence is the subject of "In the beginning," another poem having to do with the relation between matter and spirit. The first verse of the book of John to which the title phrase refers—"In the beginning was the Word, and the Word was with God, and the Word was God"—is said by Biblical authorities to refer to the initiation of the creation by God's spoken command. But Thomas uses it as if it confirmed his own feeling that even the material universe owes its existence to the creative power of language. When he was a child, Thomas said, he felt this power in words: "There they were, seemingly lifeless, made only of black and white, but out of them, out of their own being, came love and terror and pity and pain and wonder. . . . That was the time of innocence; words burst upon me unencumbered by trivial or portentous associations; words were their spring-like selves, fresh with Eden's dew as they flew out of the air."[4]

Thomas' attachment to words began with sounds; and since, like Baudelaire, he thought of reality as a *"forêt de symboles,"* he could envision an articulate nature:

> Some let me make you of the vowelled beeches,
> Some of the oaken voices, from the roots
> Of many a thorny shire tell you notes,
> Some let me make you of the water's speeches.

"In the beginning" recapitulates the creation of such a universe; its elements, if they are like words, had to be set in order. Before the coming of language, they spun chaotically in aboriginal fire, "burning ciphers in the round of space," and the natural order emerged in forms resembling language, with "the pale signature," "imprints on the water," and "a sign" left by the blood of Christ. The analogy between the order of nature and the order of language, each established by processes of selection and patterning, is beautifully stated in:

> In the beginning was the word, the word
> That from the solid bases of the light
> Abstracted all the letters of the void. . . .

Further, language constitutes consciousness, for it begins as "The word flowed up, translating to the heart/First characters of birth and death," and this awareness enables man to read his experience as if it were a verbal text. The reason for the early appearance in nature of the symbolic elements is given in the last stanza. All was created by a rational force, the "secret brain" of God, and his vision of order was "celled and soldered in the thought" before the growth of biological life had begun— "before the pitch was forking to the sun"—and before the advent of man, "The ribbed original of love."

Thomas associates language with blood, apparently on the ground that the former is necessary to spiritual life, as the latter is to biological life. Blood as the embodiment of meaningfulness appears three times in "In the beginning" in a varied but consistent extended metaphor. Rendered holy by its association with the cross and "the grail," the vessel of the Mass, it "Touched the first cloud and left a sign"; that is, passed its signifying capacity to one of the elements of nature. The metaphor also appears, in accordance with the persistence of imagery characteristic of Thomas, in "Especially when the October wind," another poem on the subject of the speaking power of nature. The poem is spoken by an inhabitant of the world resulting from the act of creation described in "In the beginning." He knows that each detail of the visible world is meaningful; there are "the meadow's signs" and the "signal grass." The experiences that invest his perceptions are "a tower of words," and the agencies of meaning —words, gestures, voices, notes, speech—appear everywhere in the familiar scenes through which he moves. Even his lifeblood is speech, "syllabic blood," and it follows that the heart, as it beats, "talks," and is "spelling in the scurry/Of chemic blood." The message offered by this articulate nature within and without is not reassuring, in spite of the beauty expressed in the supremely musical final quatrain of stanza two. What it says in the time of the October wind is a threat of hardship. The "wagging clock" and the weathercock indicate that the cycle of nature is approaching "the coming fury" of winter and its association with death, and that among the speeches of nature are "the heartless words."

The spiritual significance of the material world is accessible only to those who possess the awareness which Thomas was content to call, vaguely, "faith." Two of the 18 Poems make use of a metaphor relating this perceptiveness to waking, and spiritual indifference, or the illusion that ordinary life is the only reality, to sleep and dreams. In "When once the twilight locks no longer," the speaker, God, complains that his emissary, Jesus, failed to accomplish his mission, that he "fell asleep," and became a "poppied pickthank." "Our eunuch dreams" uses this image in attacking contemporary life for its lack of faith, comparing it to two examples of illusion: dreams and the movies.[5]

A rejected first section of "Our eunuch dreams" found in the August, 1933, notebook clarifies the metaphoric principle that night and its dreams are corrupting. It describes the spiritual dissolution and the ghostly returns that take place at nightfall, concluding with the lines, "Night of the flesh is shaken of its blood,/Night of the brain stripped of its burning bush."[6] Thus, the night deprives us equally of intelligence and of the miraculous power of faith. The dreams with which the published poem opens are, therefore, appropriately enough, sterile—"Our eunuch dreams." The quatrain following their introduction describes their dreadful work: lacking spiritual qualities, they are content with a dead shadow of love, and resurrect soulless figures of women for their brides. The actuality Thomas seems to have in mind here cannot be very different from the rendezvous of the typist and the house agent's clerk described in The Waste Land.

An illustration of the falsehood which serves the imagination "in this our age" is offered in the scene from the movies, an illusion which disappears in the daylight. Under the conditions of a life without faith, sleep and waking are no more than "two sleepings," and there is no real choice between the daytime world of "sunny gentlemen" and the night of sterile dreams. The quatrain of Part III says that illusions have won complete dominance, that the movie is inseparably pasted against the eye. The two lines "The dream has sucked the sleeper of his faith/ That shrouded men might marrow as they fly," though exceptionally obscure, seem capable of some clarification. The first line is merely a reassertion of the symbolic meaning of the dream, "sucked" being drawn from the vampire image that occasionally appears among Thomas' submerged metaphors. The faith that has been killed is belief in resurrection and immortality, "marrow" being used verbally, as Tindall has pointed out, to mean the revitalizing of the bones of the "shrouded men" who are being raised from the grave.

The final section of the poem is a call to faith in the spiritual life that transcends "our strips of stuff." The belief in resurrection, says Thomas in the image of the cock, will effect what it envisions. The image of the shots and the plates in this section is photographic, referring back by contrast to the "shots" in Part II which the characters in the movie "impose" upon the mind. Our imaginative creations, Thomas is saying, will replace those of Hollywood. The last three lines of the poem are, in comparison with the balance and refinement of most of Thomas' work, robust and insensitive. Their resonance is damped somewhat by the fact that the faith in whose name they speak is left so indefinite.

"Where once the waters of your face" supports the value of belief against the destructiveness of intellect. One of the difficulties of the poem is caused by the fact that the subject, faith or belief, masquerades behind a double metaphor. Its metaphoric equivalent is the sea, but the sea itself is addressed as if it were a person, possessing a face and "coloured lids." Once this surface confusion has been set aside, it is clear that in the first three stanzas the poet is speaking to a "wasteland" sea that at one time provided a pathway for him as if he were a ship, but has now dried up. The word "break" in the third stanza presents one of those situations in which a word possessing a satisfactory literal sense is really meant metaphorically. The lines describe the disappearance of the tides, not merely their striking against the shore; they disintegrate over the beds of weeds and leave them dry. It is a magical event, like the one in ". . . the fathomed sea/Breaks on unangled land," from "A process in the weather of the heart," where the point of the awkward "unangled" is that the breaking of the waves is caused by something other than a rugged coast. In both poems the fertilizing waters disappear because they are measured; one is "fathomed," the other "clocking." But if intellectual activity dries up the vitality of the sea, with its mermen and dolphins, the "sage magic" of faith, according to the last stanza, will restore it.

"Light breaks where no sun shines" is also about the value of faith. Instead of emphasizing the inclusion of man in the universal process, as most of the 18 Poems do, it declares that man can stand against a forbidding universe. It employs the body-earth metaphor and a series of paradoxes to state the co-existence of contraries. But, in doing so, it defines a special life-bringing role for "the fruit of man" in a universe "where no sun shines." Man offers something positive through "the waters of the heart," the glowworms in the flesh, the phallic candle, and the compassion of "the oil of tears." Even when he is dead, his spirit continues its aspiration: "Where no seed stirs/The fruit of man unwrinkles in the stars. . . ." In stanza three the process of enlightenment is described as dawning over the earth of the body, and the capacity for sympathy pours forth, unhampered by the fences or stakes of surveyors who impose limits on the earth. In stanza four the hostility of the universe is dominant, though the line, "The film of spring is hanging from the lids," promises that the time of fertility is approaching.

The final stanza of this poem is exceptional, for it employs a scene from Thomas' actual experience, as he might have described it in one of the short stories of A Portrait of the Artist as a Young Dog. Tindall has observed that the "secret lots" and "tips of thought" are garbage dumps like those Thomas saw in depression-ridden Swansea in his youth. Futile intellectuality has been thrown away in them, and now serves merely to fertilize the soil where intuitional knowledge springs up. The light of intuition comes—"blood jumps in the sun"—to illuminate the "waste allotments" littered with dead logic.[7]

III

A majority of the 18 Poems dwell upon states of conflict preceding the mystical resolution. Most of these, in turn, are somewhat more personal in tone than the other poems, for their conflicts are presented as experiences of the poet or specific characters. But most of them also open the door to the transcendence of individual identity and to a grasp of cosmic reality, either by generalizing, or through the suggestions of imagery and vocabulary. The first of the *18 Poems,* "I see the boys of summer," for example, is a dialogue between youthful representatives of the fertility principle and some wiser heads who see the inexorable balance of nature and understand that the boys have mistaken a part of experience for the whole. The boys think they can stop the natural cycle at the time of lust and pleasure, an effect spoken of as "freezing" it. This metaphor leads to the paradox that, though the boys themselves are full of heat, the effects of their actions are to produce "jacks of frost" and "frigid threads." Hence, the first section warns, in a moralizing tone uncommon in Thomas' work, that nothing good can come of the indifference and contempt the boys are displaying.

If the first section stresses the licentiousness of fertility, the boys' reply argues that there is a fertility in licentiousness. What the boys are proposing—to put it too simply—is that time must have a stop. They have in mind, not the unmoving time of the mystic vision, but a voluptuous lingering upon delectable moments—a lotos-eater's escape from necessities. Their motivation resembles that of the madman in Thomas' story, "The Mouse and the Woman." Fearing that the woman he has brought from the sea will lose her beauty, the madman decides that the time of destruction must be held back, that "winter must not appear," and that therefore the procession of the seasons, the passage of time, and the order of nature must be changed. Similarly, the boys say that they intend to "challenge" the "seasons," resist death, and spread chaos through the acts of disruption and sacrilege described in stanzas three to five. They do not see that the effects of this attempt to intervene in natural processes and to reverse spiritual realities will be pernicious.

These effects are described in the remarkable image of the unborn children who result from these lusts in the third stanza of Section I. What the children are doing as they "Split up the brawned womb's weathers,/Divide the night and day with fairy thumbs," is analogous to the destructive work of Blake's Urizen: "Times on times he divided & measur'd/Space by space in his ninefold darkness." Being the offspring of sin, they are introducing artificial divisions in the natural ones of "sun and moon" and staining their mothers with the "quartered shades" of loss of innocence. However, the boys' program is not wholly destructive; as the line "O see the poles of promise in the boys" indicates, their view is a necessary moment of error in the cyclic process. The final stanza is a brief dialogue of reconciliation between the debaters; the antagonists, speaking alternately, acknowledge their relationship, recognizing that the principle the boys represent is an element of a larger whole. The resolution is expressed in the line "O see the poles are kissing as they cross," an image which appears in the short story, "A Prospect of the Sea," as part of a heavenly vision.

One of the difficulties of this poem is attributable to the fact that the diction, even when strongly evocative subjects are at hand, seeks neutrality. As the spokesman of balance, the poet formulates a rhetoric that will favor neither side. The maintenance of this impartiality seems to require a persistent and obscurantist ambiguity, as in "fair dead" and "merry squires"; and even the substitution of a term for its opposite, so that "death" in the line "Death from a summer woman" really means, as we have observed earlier, "birth." The difficulty is inescapable in discourse about concepts for which no conventional terms exist. "Death" means not only "birth" but the whole sequence of events of which death and birth are parts. Similarly, the dead are "fair" because they were so at one time; and time, in this realm, is simultaneous, so that their past state is their present state.

"This attempt," said Robert Horan of Thomas' early style, "to surround a subject from continuously shifting levels of time, space and emotion sets up problems of perspective and chronology that cloud as often as they amplify the vision."[8] In seeking to include opposing currents of reality within single statements, Thomas often fell short—as he admitted in his letter to Treece—"in making a momentary peace with my images at the correct moment," so that enigmatic contradictions survive his craftsmanship.

A notable consequence of this persistent balancing of oppositions is the strangely detached tone pervading these poems. Strongly emotive words are paired in combinations which cancel each other out. Bursts of intense feeling are braced by calculated intricacies of construction and are forced into shape by a disciplined literalism. Detachment is, of course, appropriate to mysticism. But it is shown to be a matter of style as well as vision by the fact that even poems that fall short of self-transcendence are severely disciplined in their language. In "The force that through the green fuse drives the flower," (the most celebrated of Thomas' early poems), the speaker sees the duality of natural forces but complains that he is influenced only by their destructive side. Much of the poem's effectiveness arises from the magnificently controlled structural device of making each of the four stanzas a variant of a single refrain, maintaining an identical rhythm and a slightly varied syntactical pattern in all of them. This formal repetitiveness stresses the fact that the four stanzas are assertions of the same thought, that the poet is a victim of the system of nature. In addition, there is a complex development of structural relationships within each stanza, including repetitions, parallels ("flower . . . green age"), alliteration ("drives . . . dries"), contrasts ("red blood . . . wax"), and antitheses ("water . . . quicksand").

This tight structure conveys two balanced ideas: the kinship between nature and the speaker, who are subjected to the same forces, and the duality of these forces, alternately creative and destructive. The first three lines of each stanza are devoted to these thoughts, and the last two to the point that the speaker feels his relationship to be with whatever suffers destruction. The identifications magically transform both the body and its environment into the transparent films of mystical reality, so that the destructive energies of water, wind, quicklime, and worm pass uninterrupted between them. The first three lines of the fourth stanza reverse the pattern; they move in a negative, rather than a positive, direction. They say that love does not share the speaker's fate because, though it may be wounded, the bleeding has the therapeutic effect of treatment by a "leech." On the other hand, "And I am dumb to tell a weather's wind/How time has ticked a heaven round the stars" suggests that the human notion of time has, within its limited concept of death, a limited concept of immortality—"a heaven" rather than "heaven" itself. In an early draft of the poem, "a weather's wind" read "the timeless sun," offering a contrast between "timeless" and "time" which is lost in the final version.[9]

This poem is particularly interesting because it provides a

context in which some of Thomas' submerged metaphors achieve evocative effects without the support of their associations. "Blasts," "wintry fever," "wax," and "sucks" are each, as we have seen, parts of metaphors operative in *18 Poems* as a whole; yet it is not necessary to infer them intellectually to feel their force. In this poem, therefore, Thomas has succeeded better than elsewhere in fashioning his special idiom into poetry that speaks directly, without the intervention of analysis and explication.

"My hero bares his nerves" is another poem which frames a private spiritual problem in spare, economical statement. Its subject is the conflict between two impulses condemned to share a single consciousness: the desires for pleasure and for spiritual awareness. The "hero" is the poet's creative self, who, finding that the nerves, head, and heart that he has in common with his physical counterpart are monopolized respectively by sloth, spiritual indifference, and lust, takes control and turns the body toward the possibilities of imaginative vision. The poem is organized according to the machine metaphor, for the body is conceived (in a rather confused manner, to be sure) as an electrical contraption: the brain is the source of energy, the nerves, the wires. Since the brain is dominated by sleep, Thomas' emblem of spiritual indifference, the poetry emerging from it through the nerves can express only the pain of unfulfilled love. Seeking the source of the trouble, the poet finds within himself a situation symbolizing the dominance of physical desire, his heart treading the beach of flesh, a scene whose resemblance to Botticelli's "Venus" seems to be insisted upon. He acts upon this diagnosis by supplying a "secret heat," an awareness of the "mortal error" of the human state and of the scene of the Crucifixion, which redeems it. His loyalty passes from the "mortal ruler," or spine of human pride which supports him in the first stanza, to the "hunger's emperor," Christ, the man of sorrows.

The final line is, of course, a shock. It is defensible as a metaphoric expression of the "hero's" purgation of the waste matter of his earlier life, and the image of the feces suggests the maggot in the stool. We should not be mistaken, however, if we detected, as one of the impulses behind this indecency in a religious context, a disposition to outrage convention. Thomas

enjoyed attacking ordinary moral standards as a means of en-
larging the reader's tolerance. Considering this motivation, it is
perhaps irrelevant to say that the image is aesthetically unsatisfactory because it leaps from nowhere and fails to continue the
well-constructed metaphoric logic of the poem.

IV

"If I were tickled by the rub of love" differs from most of *18
Poems* in being a personal statement in a form resembling a dramatic monologue spoken by a fairly well-defined character in
a sufficiently specific emotional difficulty. Olson, in his persuasive reading of this poem in *The Poetry of Dylan Thomas*
(37-41), describes its speaker as "a modern Hamlet" whose feelings about such fundamental aspects of life as birth, growth,
love, and death are agonizingly divided between desire and
fear. In the last stanza he decides to arm himself against these
doubts by limiting himself to the human and the actual.

The remarkable diversity of uses to which Thomas puts the
words "rub" and "tickle" in this poem, making structural devices
of them and their associations, is a good instance of his metaphoric virtuosity. Both words have unblushing sexual associations and
form a metaphor in which all the processes of life are one term;
sex is the other. Thus, to consider the problems of sex and love
is to consider the problems of life.

The metaphor is developed by exploiting the two words for
their ambiguities, so that we see the entwined contradictions in
them and in the experiences to which they refer. The "rub" of
tactile sexual pleasure is also in the last two stanzas the Eliza-
bethan "rub" of troubles or obstacles. To the recognized meaning of "tickle" the poem adds another, one approximating "to
evoke a genuine emotional reaction." Hence, the conditional
statements of the first four stanzas are essentially complaints
that the speaker has not experienced love. "The only rub that
tickles," the only stimulus to which he really responds, is fear
of death.

The first line of the last stanza, "And what's the rub? Death's
feather on the nerve?" is typical of the many junctures in *18
Poems* which lead the reader to feel that he is in the presence of

an invisible, elaborate network of associations. "Death's feather" is a familiar eccentricity of this volume. Perhaps the basis of the association, as G. S. Fraser has said, is the use of a feather as a test for breathing when someone appears to be dead. But the feather is also linked, quite unexpectedly, with "tickles"; hence, it is not only a symbol of death but, within the context of the poem it is a stimulus of living feelings. Thus, the feather is a metaphoric node combining the contraries of life and death; and it is related to them, not through arbitrary symbolic associations, but through the strangely literal, even naïve perception that it stirs up life by tickling and tells of death by lying still. One of these associations is jocose, the other grave; but this incongruity does not weaken the image.

Neither the problems nor the conclusion of the speaker in this poem has much to do with mysticism. His suffering arises from an adolescent distrust of the necessities of the human condition, and the program he announces at the end is a conscious and rational one. The comparatively conventional rhetoric achieves some remarkable locutions, such as "devil in the loin," "daft with the drug that's smoking in a girl," and "Man be my metaphor." But the prevailing diction and imagery belong to the larger framework of Thomas' mysticism, and they reflect the duality, timelessness, and other special conditions of absolute vision. The apple, the flood, the crossed sticks of war, and "my Jack of Christ" are all religious symbols with ambiguous implications. "The itch of man upon the baby's thigh," the paired lovers who will emerge from impulses that lead to the scribbling of *graffiti,* and "the worm beneath the nail" are compressions of time which present the potential side by side with the actual.

There is exceptionally close continuity between the imagery of the poems "If I were tickled by the rub of love," and "From love's first fever to her plague," for the plum, the mother's fertile side, and the bud forking the eye are all repeated. Further, the second poem may be considered a continuation of the first: it is a spiritual autobiography by one who has passed through doubts and conflicts and who is now able to review them and to grasp the essential unity that underlies the apparent diversity of experience. The first stanza describes existence as it appears to the embryonic consciousness, a single, undifferentiated unity—"All world was one, one windy nothing." In the second stanza, thought begins to make elementary distinctions in the child's mind. The imagery of the winds in the third stanza recalls Thomas' occasional use of the wind to mean the "inner weather" of thought and feeling. Hence, the synesthetic merging of the senses in

> And the four winds, that had long blown as one,
> Shone in my ears the light of sound,
> Called in my eyes the sound of light,

reflects the awareness that their reports, in spite of their differing qualities, pertain to the single experience of life. The imagery of maturation in this stanza is unexpectedly effective; in particular, the line "Each golden grain spat life into its fellow" is a remarkably vital rendering of the microscopic phenomena of fertility and growth that are continuously present in Thomas' biological mysticism.

The fifth stanza exhibits the special fervor Thomas felt toward language. The development of speech is an important stage in the speaker's growth, not only because he is a poet, but because, as we have seen, expression in mythic consciousness is creative. The relation of language and life is brilliantly embodied in Thomas' ironic phrase for the beginning of wisdom, "the first declension of the flesh." Expression compels him "to twist the shapes of thought/Into the stony idiom of the brain"; that is, to force the anomalous creations of the mind into the resistant, insufficiently flexible form of language. These lines are an eloquent testimonial to the difficulty the mythic mind has in finding a medium for its ideas.

On the other hand, in learning speech, he also learned "To shade and knit anew the patch of words/Left by the dead. . . ." Through this somber metaphor Thomas projects the view that language grows tattered with use and that it is the poet's function to reconstitute it, not by simplifying, but by adding new threads and colors and by increasing its complexity. The last two lines of the stanza are a digression on the dead, but they are relevant to the subject of language, for death is the end of the organized perception of reality made possible by language. What the maggots are doing is reversing the development of language, replacing the "name" with their inarticulate "X."

The final stanza is a remarkable poetic summation of the effects of the development of consciousness on metaphysical theory. Intuition, expressed through the metaphors of communication that persist throughout the poem, taught the speaker that the diversity of experience was merely a disguised form of the essential unity. Birth forced him to recognize the polarity of the universe, and the requirements of living fractioned existence into many unrelated parts: "From the divorcing sky I learnt the double,/The two-framed globe that spun into a score. . . ." is a terse, objective account of the passage from innocence to experience. But the final stage is a return to an awareness of the singleness of life: "One sun, one manna, warmed and fed."

The "fever" and "plague" of the first line are related to the key metaphor based on the idea that the fertility of the universe is a disease contracted from a divine source. The association itself is, of course, far from new ("After life's fitful fever he sleeps well"); but Thomas' literal and detailed development of it produces some original, even cryptic, imagery. He seems chiefly occupied with two specific resemblances between "fever" and "life": both are warm; both can be transmitted. A more general resemblance, the fact that both lead to death, qualifies the metaphor as one of the "warring images" that embraces contradictions. Hence, in this poem, love, the reproductive force, begins with conception as "fever" and it ends, having arrived at the extreme of its development, as contagious "plague," with the generation of new life. The image appears not only in such locutions as the "wintry fever" of life in "The force that through the green fuse," and "the cross of fever" which symbolizes the transmission of spiritual energy in "When, like a running grave," but also in such extensions as "power was contagious in my birth" in "I dreamed my genesis," and "contagious man," in "All all and all the dry worlds lever."

The group of images in "such a bud/As forks my eye" from the final stanza appears also in "If I were tickled by the rub of love," where the context suggests that "bud" is phallic. "Fork" is one of Thomas' most common and most ingenious neologisms. Its frequent appearances in unpublished as well as published poems make it possible to distinguish two antithetical ranges of meaning for it. It often relates to a divergence signifying growth or budding, such as the branching of a tree, as in "forked out the bearded apple" in "Incarnate devil," where the budding of the Tree of Knowledge is being described. The ultimate source of this sense is probably the forked root of the mandrake. But in an early unpublished poem, the word occurs twice, as verb and as noun, referring to the pitchfork used by the devil and his henchmen. (This is the same passage where the important image of the devil's scissors appears, and this contiguity suggests that the two bear a relationship to each other.)[10] This meaning is present in contexts like "such a bud/As forks my eye" which involve transfixing or penetration. "Forks" seems to have been attractive to Thomas as a word that could encompass implications of fertility on the one hand and sin and destruction on the other. The two opposing connotations fit together when "fork" is used to mean the loins. Hence, the lines "A million minds gave suck to such a bud/As forks my eye," is simply a statement about the inheritance of generative powers, though it is crowded with antithetical effects, and with images that efface each other.

Most of the formidable obscurities of "When, like a running grave" have yielded to the irresistible analyses of Olson and Tindall, who—though they do not quite agree about the poem's general sense—unite in seeing it as a meditation on the nature of love and its relation to death, in the same vein as "If I were tickled by the rub of love." Tindall thinks the speaker is expressing fear that he will experience sexual failure before death overtakes him; Olson sees the problem as a rivalry between physical and intellectual approaches to love, which explains why the poem is addressed to "head and heart." Among the many specific images upon which the two explicators disagree is the defunct turtle dove in the first stanza. Tindall thinks it is involved in sexual activity, but Olson believes the image represents the intellectualization of love.

Much of the imagery in the poem belongs to Thomas' familiar iconography; the candles are related to the waxen flesh metaphor, the "summer feather" is the threat of death, the "bud of Adam" is the phallus, and the sickness of life metaphor stands behind the statement that the wind "contages" all men with the cough. The "nitric stain" of the fifth stanza is one of Thomas' repeated symbols. Not surprisingly, he uses acid as a representative of destruction; but it also acquires magical qualities as a potion of mortality. In the short story, "The Lemon," the Moreau-like vivisectionist uses an "acid" to pervert, nourish, and ultimately destroy the victims of his experiments. An unusual feature of the poem is the presence of another character in addition to the speaker, "Cadaver," the personification of the body which represents, in spite of its name, a positive capacity for physical passion, as well as inevitable death.

The distinctive quality of "When like a running grave" is the macabre gaiety Tindall has pointed out. In spite of the fact that its dominant subject is death, many of the puns, images, and epithets have a rakish air, a consistency of tone which is in itself uncommon among these early poems. The image of death pursuing the speaker over the racetrack, in a path forming a zero or nothing, which is proposed in the first line and completed in the last stanza, has its witty side—as has Olson's explanation of the "virgin o" as a buttonhole in a shroud whose shape is symbolic of an empty life.

The amused self-deprecation of "Chaste and the chaser, man with a cockshut eye" recalls such autobiographical figures as the frustrated hero of "One Warm Saturday" and Samuel Bennet in "Adventures in the Skin Trade." The poem is, in fact, a prefiguring of the notion of himself which Thomas was to evolve from the various problems of love, death, and creation explored in these poems. He was to see himself as a victim of the ironies of the dialectic universe, one who attached a desperate importance to ephemeral satisfactions but was constantly being left defeated and in ridiculous positions by intractable realities.

V

The exceptionally complex "My world is pyramid" identifies conception with death, first through the actions of the parents, then through the speech of the embryo itself. It is apparent from this poem that the act of generation, being sinful, has destructive spiritual aspects. It is presented as a process in which each of the parents divides himself, yielding half his spirit, so that the "bisected shadows" can be unified into "the salt unborn." The second stanza shows that this sacrifice impairs the parents; each now suffers diminution, "For half of love was planted in the lost,/And the unplanted ghost." They survive, in the third stanza, as a single cripple, wandering in a grotesque seascape of symbols of sin. The last two lines of the stanza employ the image of the vampire, and the superstition of exorcism connected with it. The sleepers, or sinners, in Thomas' association, are having stakes driven through their hearts, so that they will not rise to haunt the living. Stanza four reiterates the fact that the parents were wounded or split in the act of procreation; "the wild pigs' wood," the scene of their lust, appears in one of Thomas' rejected poems.[11] "What colour is glory?" is one of the unanswerable questions asked by the children in a first draft of "Why east wind chills,"[12] and the parents ask it out of fear and confusion. Their anguish penetrates to heaven, to the divine tailor whose presence controls the imagery here. But there is no answer from the "ghost," the spirit they have engendered.

The child, who speaks in Part II, testifies that the world he has been born into seems to be a house of death, like the pyramid of a pharaoh surrounded by a desert, in which he lies as a mummy. His flesh seems to have no reality; he feels that he is no more than a "padded mummer," actor as well as mummy, and that in the "Egypt's armour" of his physical being he can find only bone and the "parhelion" or mock sun of the blood. He feels, in a rapid change of metaphoric context, that he is destined for war, where men make sacrifices comparable to that of Calvary. The materials of the body are traced, in the third stanza, wandering through the waters and soils of the earth; and it will be found that these journeys are governed by the "straws" of chance, or lack of faith. The child realizes that the parents, "the fellow halves," have been his victims as they wander through the sterile "casting tides." It is not surprising, therefore, that heaven breathes scandal while the child, "the unborn devil" carries on his masquerade, "binding my angel's hood." In the final stanza the child, reverting to the questions asked by the parents, confirms their despair; he asserts that the life they made their sacrifices to give him is a living death.

"I fellowed sleep" offers an allegorical glimpse of transcendental reality at the end of a spiritual journey. The poem is an evaluation of two methods of beginning the struggle for spiritual vision: escape into detachment, or "sleep," and acceptance of material reality. An earlier draft of the poem has a different first line, and mentions the figure of the father in the last stanza of the published poem, but limits the narrative to the spiritual adventure of the speaker.[13] The present first line, "I fellowed sleep who kissed me in the brain," was borrowed from the same notebook, where it introduces a poem on the destructive and stultifying power of sleep. It is clear, therefore, that the "second ground" to which sleep carries the narrator is a realm of sorrow because it is a world of illusion, only a little distance above the earth, and still "far from the stars." The companion he encounters here explains the nature of the place in the dialogue of the third stanza, and also tells him that the figures he sees are not angels but victims of illusion without real existence who disappear before the breath of reality.

Left alone, the speaker rids himself of these examples of spiritual failure. He is then ready for the genuine illumination offered by "the matter of the living air" as it tells him that ordinary life is an inferior existence, and that a better one awaits him in another realm: "How light the sleeping on this soily star,/How deep the waking in the worlded clouds."

This "waking" does not involve alienation from material reality. The vision, says the speaker, is "spelt" with "a hand and hair," with emblems of the living organism; its field consists of "worlded" clouds, not of mere vapors. Further, the pathway to the sun is "the hours' ladder" whose rungs are the blessings and vicissitudes of earthly life; and it is "monkeyed"—as Tindall has suggested—because it includes the steps of evolutionary development. Hence, the way to transcendence lies through experience and suffering, a long and difficult journey, as the vision of the poet's father scrambling up the ladder shows.

It has never been observed that "All all and all the dry worlds lever," the last of the *18 Poems*, is the most perfect representative of Thomas' early poetic style. It manipulates

Thomas' private vocabulary of images to form a disciplined, intricate avowal of the interdependence of fertility and death within the universe of his vision. Each of its six stanzas contains two sentences exactly three lines long, and each is formed, not on rhyme, but on the more subtle consonant rhyme. Perfectly controlled, this poem is terse and direct, and sparing even of syntax; most of it consists of appositional phrases naming the symbolic manifestations of the forces which are its subject. This repetition culminates in the mystic transport of the final stanza, with its exclamation and concluding series of asyntactical phrases.

The poem deals with the human body and the flower as symbols of generative power, making use of language and imagery which also bring forward the balancing destructive forces they harbor. The "dry worlds" in the first line are (as the rest of the poem makes clear) metaphoric representatives of the bodies of lovers; here they act as "levers," that is, means of transmitting the energy symbolized by oil and lava, and thus animating the earth, "stage of the ice." In the second part of the stanza, the flower is a prediction of coming life contained within an otherwise scorched and barren earth.

The sequence of contradictory epithets applied in the second stanza to the body, "my naked fellow," is a mingling of allusions to creative and destructive capacities. "Dug of the sea, the glanded morrow," with its implications of suckling and growth, contrasts with "worm in the scalp." This duality is crowded into the adjectives "staked and fallow." Both imply that the body is earth and say, on the one hand, that it is measured out, ready for sowing; on the other, that it is pierced by the vampire's stake and unproductive. The reversed sentence concluding Part I repeats the statement that the lovers will revivify what is dead and evil.

In Part II the poet assures his body that it has nothing to fear from life and procreation. Part III begins with an announcement of the sexual union that brings the lovers together. But in embracing each other they also embrace the past and future each of them contains; they have "their arms/Round the griefs of the ages," like the lovers in "In my craft or sullen art." Thus, the implication of new life—"All that shapes from the caul and suckle"—and the experience of physical caressing bring the lovers

within the immemorial order of life: "Square in these worlds"—
the lovers—"the mortal circle." The final stanza celebrates this
consummation, making use of such conventional symbols of
generation as light and flame and of such images from Thomas'
private repertoire as the fertile grave and the oil.

In "All all and all" Thomas is exceptionally successful in using
the special images of his mysticism. The lovers' bodies whose
fertility contains and animates "all" are identified as machines,
in accordance with his association. Hence, they act as "levers,"
the sinful love which besets them is wittily called "the flesh's
lock and vice," the desires which turn each of them to the object
of love are "screws" manipulated by the divine engineer; and
they make love through "mechanical flesh." This association operates throughout the poem, and is one of its main points of
departure; it is particularly apparent in the first stanza of Part
II, where the various symbols of reproductive energies mingle
the fertile and the mechanical. Being a machine, the body
contains "synthetic blood" and is composed of "ribbing metal."
The things it seems to fear are all implements related to growth,
fertility, or energy which do their work by violent means: the
"tread" of the primitive threshing floor (or of the barnyard),
the grinding of the seed in a mill, the trigger and flint that spark
the explosion of fertility. The scythe is the "bridal blade,"
because it represents the harvest; but the "scythe-eyed raven"
in the next stanza stands for sin and recalls the doctrine of the
sharp instrument within Thomas' metaphor.

The poem closes with a merging of the two symbols of the
dialectic of fertility and mortality which Thomas sees as the
pattern of life: the flower, and the embracing lovers, who form
a "coupled bud." The last stanza consists of two formless exclamations. The first accepts the flower of love and growth
as "the flesh's vision." The last accepts it as a cosmic symbol,
springing from the contradictory elements of the earth and embodying the continuity of life and death.

CHAPTER 4

Twenty-five Poems

I

MOST of the poems in Thomas' second volume of verse are comparable in style to *18 Poems* and exhibit good continuity with the earlier volume. Since many of them are based on drafts written before the publication of *18 Poems*, it is not surprising that they should reflect the same cosmic conditions: the dialectic of nature, the simultaneity of time, the correspondence of spiritual and material worlds, and the symmetry of life and death.[1] The metaphoric associations of *18 Poems* are also prominent in the later volume; these include the identification of man and nature, of flesh and metal, of body and universe, and the imagery of warfare, the Bible, and the bearer of the sharp instrument.

However, the revisions Thomas made in 1935 and 1936 of drafts written in 1933 were often extensive, and they produced decisive improvements. It would, therefore, be a mistake to think that the later work is in all respects indistinguishable from the earlier. *Twenty-five Poems* does, as a matter of fact, create a somewhat different impression from *18 Poems*. For one thing, the individual pieces have a wider range of intelligibility. There are at least two passages—in addition to the "Altarwise by owl-light" sequence, which is properly considered separately— that display a more radical disruption of syntax and imagery than any found in *18 Poems*. On the other hand, the new volume contains the first poem Thomas published in his maturity which is free—or nearly free—of any obscurity whatever, "This bread I break."

Ralph Maud has warned that the less congested poems of *Twenty-five Poems* and of *The Map of Love* (such as "Ears in the turrets hear" and "This bread I break") cannot be said to show that Thomas simplified his style as he matured, for they are early compositions.² But *Twenty-five Poems* does show, in other ways, the beginnings of Thomas' later manner. Some of the pieces depart from the introspective approach to cosmic truth which is the dominant theme of *18 Poems*. The view that the language of poetry arises directly from symbolic nature—found in "In the beginning" and in "Especially when the October wind" —is developed in *Twenty-five Poems* into a number of observations about myths, legends, and poetry that consider external as well as private realities. At least three of the poems in the second volume are about the poet's reactions to other people, themes of an entirely different class from those of *18 Poems;* and these three anticipate Thomas' turning outward in his later poems toward such subjects as his aunt's funeral, the landscape, and his relations with his wife and children.

"Foster the light" is among the poems in this volume which continue both the vision and poetic style of *18 Poems*. In the first three stanzas the poet calls upon himself to resolve the conflicts of the dialectic universe by acknowledging the domination of light, a familiar symbol—in Thomas as well as in other poets—of mystic illumination. As we have observed, he had used the imagery of dark and light to represent the contest of the spirit in an unpublished poem, "Twenty One," written about a year before "Foster the light" itself.³ The veiling of the moon and the acceptance of the snowman's view of the world in the first stanza of "Foster the light" are metaphoric warnings against the forfeiture of mystic insight. The conflict that calls for Thomas' aid in the second stanza lies between barrenness and fertility; Thomas urges himself to "farmer in time of frost," to render the world fruitful through an act of will so inclusive that it will make him considerate of even so unlikely a case of fertility as "cockerel's eggs." The result will be, as the last line of the stanza says, that the seeds sown in his youth will become, through their continued fertility, a "vegetable century."

In the third stanza the resolution of conflict between contraries is expressed through a number of musical metaphors. The gestation of this imagery also occurs in an unpublished poem written in 1933.⁴ This poem, an autobiographical description of the problems of childhood and youth, speaks of a period of five years devoted to attempts to order the chaos of life.

The musical image is explicit, involving the jarring sounds of a badly played piano. Mystic reconciliation is a harmony, and the contradictions of life, when fitted together, result in music. The resolution of the discords of the universe is the music associated with the "ninnies' choir," "the singing cloud," and the "mandrake music" of "Foster the light."

This confidence in the benign orderliness of the universe, continues the fourth stanza, will transcend even death. The assertion is put first in the form of a command, and then of an observation to the effect that the tides of the seas will continue even after the poet and his love have died. In the metaphors of this stanza death and the sea exchange idioms; Thomas speaks of his own death as a departure aboard a ship, as he does in "I, in my intricate image"; and the graveyard where his love will lie is "a cross-boned drift," a sea of disordered bones and crosses. The denial that the sea's tides can be reversed, on the other hand, takes the form of turning "cockwise"; that is, with the irresponsible veering of the "bow-and-arrow birds" of weather vanes found on churches near graveyards.

In addressing God, the final stanza asserts the holiness of nature, for the cargo of the ark consisted of "his coloured doubles." The form of deliverance Thomas calls for has some interesting implications. He asks God to reciprocate his own imaginative transformation of the moon into "a merry manshape" by making "the world of me," implying that the poetic imagination is an attribute of God. By identifying the moon with man, Thomas has diminished and humanized it; but God, if he is to perform an imaginative feat proportional to his powers, must extend the poet into a cosmos, "make the world of me."

In spite of its comparative clarity and directness, "This bread I break," which is an early poem written in 1933, is fully committed to the mysticism prevailing in the poetry of this period. It is an intricate, systematic statement about a spiritually charged physical universe whose identities flow into one another, but the scope of allusion to the special conditions of such a universe is limited, as it happens, to comparatively accessible associations. The biological processes that weave all matter together are shaped into a striking vision of the cruelty of the natural cycle. Oat and grape, formed by the same elements in which "Man in the day" has his being, are counterparts of his body; in harvesting and consuming them, he is therefore performing a strange, inescapable act of cannibalism. In the first stanza, the speaker is the diner; in the last, the victim at the feast. Tracing the cycle of nature, he discovers his own destruction in the destruction he brings to oat and grape, thus confronting the brotherhood of all life.

This discovery is beautifully balanced on the ambiguity of "This flesh you break, this blood you let/Make desolation in the vein . . . ." For, although these words follow the metaphors established in the previous stanza and are about bread and wine, when they are reread in the light of the poem's conclusion, the literal force of "this blood you let" breaks through; and with it appears a second meaning for the passage as a whole.

This meaning is, in fact, the original one the lines bore in the draft which appears in two slightly differing versions dated December 24, 1933, in the notebook begun in August, 1933. The first draft is entitled "Breakfast Before Execution," a title indicating that the two lines in question are spoken by a prisoner who tells his executioners that their action in killing him is, like the reaping of oat and grape, a violation of the holiness of life. The original version of the concluding lines accuses the executioners of eating God's bread and drinking from His cup. The last line, "My wine you drink, my bread you snap," expressed a religious idea in the second draft, for "wine" read "sins," and "snap" was "break." By eliminating the title, Thomas transformed the poem from a dramatic monologue to a lyric, and by eliminating the pious tone of the ending in favor of the savage and self-accusatory "snap," he changed it from a Christian poem to a statement of his own austere nature mysticism.

II

The first poem of *Twenty-five Poems*, "I in my intricate image," is the climactic work of Thomas' early period, for it develops the associations, metaphors, and themes of *18 Poems* into a full, complex rendering of the vision of man in the cosmos with which the first volume is occupied. Because it ranges widely over the realities of Thomas' universe, the subject of "I, in my intricate image" is difficult to define. Tindall thinks the poem is about the power of poetic imagery; Olson has said that it is "a meditation on death." Both of these themes have important places in the poem, yet they, together with the theme of the duality of man and nature, seem to be only parts of a larger subject that might be stated as the immortal companionship of matter and spirit.

Originally published in the August-September, 1935, issue of *New Verse* under the title "A Poem in Three Parts," it consists of three distinct, though related, sections. The first is about the poet's birth and development. The soil and vegetation are its dominant metaphoric background. The second is about death, represented metaphorically as a return to the sea; the third, about resurrection. These parts are linked to each other by a number of sustained images extended through the poem as a whole, or through long passages of it, forming a more or less continuous source of allusions and associations. There are also localized metaphors distinct from the larger metaphoric structure, such as those of the spinner in the second stanza and the phonograph at the end of Part II.

The poem is properly read, not as a general observation or meditation, but a narrative of spiritual development. If it seems to lack narrative movement, that is because, like most of Thomas' early poems, it sets aside conventional notions of chronology in order to project a vision of a timeless universe. The past tense of the end does not indicate a time earlier than the present tense of the beginning, where the duality of the poet and his universe is proposed. The poet is a "metal phantom"; that is, a supernatural core encased in the "minerals" of the body's armor, an insubstantial spirit linked to hard flesh. Brass, in Thomas' imagery, is identified with passion, as is suggested by these lines from a poem in the February, 1933, notebook: "In me man and woman's brazen,/Yet have I played the eunuch to all passion. . . ."[5]

The speaker's two identities are in conflict; the "brassy orator" can find peace only by "laying" the ghost of the spirit. But the poet is also "Cadaver's masker" of the final stanza, a masquerader wearing the costume of life over the inward reality of ultimate death. He inhabits a world that also has a double aspect, a "twin world" which weighs him morally in its "scales" as he "strides on two levels," stepping in its uneven balances. Having thus formulated his situation, the poet returns to origins in the second stanza. Here we have an impressive lyrical rendering of the biological processes that link man to the soil; the spring, personified as a spinner, disentangles the fibers of nature and weaves them into a new fabric that becomes man. The third stanza exploits ingenious parallels with the second to form a contrasting statement of the means by which the poet duplicates this creation, fashioning a spiritual double of his physical self to bring forth the "twin miracle."

But it is "the fortune of manhood," continues the fourth stanza, to lose spiritual awareness—"no death more natural." The man who lacks his shadow, the ox, the picture of the devil, "the wooden insect," "the tree of nettles," and "the glass bed of grapes" are all emblems of existence after this loss. The section ends as the double self, now spoken of in the third person plural as "the invalid rivals," leaves the hospital of life for a voyage which, while it will end in shipwreck and death, will also lead to rebirth and so become a "sea-blown arrival."

The narrative tone of the poem emerges clearly at the beginning of Part II, where the voyage seems to be preceded by a walk through a landscape exhibiting the joyous energies of nature. Then, without transition and with an astounding lack of emphasis, comes death, represented both by immersion in the sea and by the traditional dust—"As they dive, the dust settles," —so that the two aspects of the poet's self become the "riderless dead," turning, as they lie in the water, with the motion of the waves stirred up by "the seabear and mackerel." The parenthesis which interrupts the narrative here develops the Atropos figure, by ingenious associations, to present death as a scene in an operating room. The killer is a surgeon, bearing the sharp, bright instrument; and the bodily orifices he opens are graves, so that the operation becomes an "antiseptic funeral." The second stanza of the parenthesis sarcastically calls for the "black patrol" of the clergy to attend the death, and it concludes, in spite of the sexton's gloomy observation, with an allusion to Lazarus and the approaching resurrection. Since the drowning is really a rebirth, it is accompanied by the sound of bells rung in the sea; death and consecration are mingled in a harmonious "Dead Sea scale."

The section concludes with an inventive rendering of the mystical view of existence through the image of a phonograph. Thomas, who matches the members of his grotesque pairing detail for detail, carries the process to such unexpected lengths that the final total equivalence acquires enough momentum to carry conviction. The spindle at the center of the turntable is the sea; the record that it turns is the land; the "lightning" of the needle "dazzles" the record as it recites its trivial account of mortal life. But while this action is going on, the "circular world" of the turntable seems, to the eye at least, to be immobilized in the single moment of the mystic's eternity.

The general import of the obscure pronouncements and invocation of the first stanza of Part III is that the dead twins must endure rebirth. Their heavenly counterpart, "a double angel," say the last two lines, will rise from the inhospitable sea bottom, as surprising as a tree on the barren island of Aran. It is interesting to observe here that in Thomas' view, flesh and spirit are both immortal, so that the resurrected self retains its dual identity. In the second stanza, the mortal twins are asked to endure the infliction of death by a weapon that fuses attributes of a church steeple and Jacob's ladder into an instrument of aspiration—"a stick of folly." The last three lines of this stanza are so obscure that even their syntax is hard to determine. Perhaps the hill of smoke and the valley of drug addiction are images of earthly confusion. Perhaps the "iron mile" is a steeple forming a track for the minor vision which will enable it to reach heaven and become a major one. Perhaps the sunken Hamlet is the divided poet, now drowned in the sea of deliverance and lying on God's soil. "Coral" in other poems—notably in the related poem "It is the sinner's dust-tongued bell"—is a sacred substance, the solid deposit of the holy sea.

The continued invocation in the third stanza urges the twins to accept mortal death and to give up the struggles of flesh and love now that they find themselves, ironically, in "the bed of eels." In the last three stanzas, some of the metaphoric relationships that have been developed throughout the poem come to a climax; others are puzzling and offer tempting, if dangerous, ground for speculation. It seems clear that in "the pincers of the boiling circle," the sea and the surgeon's "instrument" are combined into a destructive figure. But what is to be said of the action of the poet, who, seeming now to have recovered his unity, says that, in his spiritual fervor, he "clawed out the crocodile"? The crocodile lives in fertile mud; he was worshiped by the Egyptians because he was supposed to reach a great age; perhaps these facts mean that he represents the vitality of nature, with which man is now identified.

The fifth stanza is clearly about the duality of time; destructive of one form of physical existence, it produces the "sea-hatched skull" and leads man, dressed in the hospital gown of the patient, to lament the loss of his body at the "antiseptic funeral." But it is also the "flying grail" that brings him to the "hourless houses" of eternity and renders him "all-hallowed." The final stanza is a brilliant recapitulation of the action of the poem through compressed but not unintelligible imagery. The physical man who concealed death within himself was conquered by the sea of death; but the lines "My ghost in his metal neptune/Forged in man's mineral" suggest, by exploiting a meaning of "forged," used in the line repeated from the second line of the poem, that physical man is only a spurious imitation of the spirit. He is "metal neptune"—flesh of the sea. The last two lines complete the narrative of resurrection by reverting to two of the poem's repeated metaphors—the sea whose energies are both creative and destructive, and "heaven's hill," a triumphant counterpart of the many high places mentioned in the poem.

The imagery of high places is a good illustration of the poetic resources Thomas has woven into the dense rhetorical fabric of this poem. It illustrates, also, the passive ingenuity involved in using an image to "let it breed another, let that image contradict the first . . . and let them all, within my imposed formal limits, conflict."[6] Beginning with the church spire as an emblem of holiness, Thomas inventively varies the notion of height, giving it contrasting forms. The "steeplejack tower" in Part I is a secular spire, the unimaginative utilitarian symbol of a life without spirit; the "country pinnacle" at the beginning of Part II, where the dual self meets the pleasures of nature, is the climax of earthly joy. And the "seastuck towers" and the small group of images relating to Jacob's ladder in Part III are counterparts of the church spire that appear in the life after death. But, not content with this image and its variants, Thomas lets it breed

another, contradictory one. (Or perhaps the process of derivation
worked in the opposite direction). In Part II the church spire
appears underwater as "the steeple of spindrift" where it is
associated with the bell that rings while the dual selves are
drowning. The image of the sunken church—which may well
have been suggested by the ringing of a bell buoy, whose notes,
sounding incongruously over the water, seem to turn the open
sea into a church—is persistent, though unobtrusive in other
poems. It appears, more fully developed, in "It is the sinner's
dust-tongued bell," where it is the dominant trope, so that the
sea as a whole is transformed into a sacred element. A child
is born in "a holy room in a wave," the energy of the sea assumes
sacramental power—"a whirlpool drives the prayerwheel"—and
the underwater bell ringing from a sunken church tower is
heard, just as it is in "I, in my intricate image."

The repetition of the word "intricate" is the hardly discern-
ible shadow of another family of associations. In "Then was my
neophyte," whose images are closely related to those of "I, in my
intricate image," the perilous sea is compared to a labyrinth. It
threatens death, but it also reverses itself to act as the source
of life. This labyrinthine turning makes it "the intricate sea-
whirl"; renders death "the intricate manhood of ending"; and
makes man himself, who is compounded of physical and spiritual
elements, and is designed to meet this complex end, an "intricate
image." The same notion seems to have "bred," through Thomas'
methods of association, the odd insistence in the parenthesis
about the surgeon that the turnkey, death, is "spiral," and that
the graves of the bodily openings are "corkscrew" shapes imitat-
ing the plan of the labyrinth. The Grand Guignol quality of
these images is essential to their effect, but they are not mere
irresponsible grotesques: no less essential is their function as
parts of an imposing fabric of consistent metaphoric thought.

The word "scales," which occurs in four different contexts in
the poem, illustrates Thomas' use of homonyms whose ambiguities can be exploited to bring together divergent areas of meaning. "The scales of this twin world" in the first stanza are, of
course the balances of weight and judgment; the "Dead Sea
scale" of Part II is Thomas' fancy of the funeral tocsin sounded
under the destructive sea; the "scaling" in the second line of

Part III seems to mean that the dead twins are climbing the towers at the water's edge, as they have climbed the contrasting "country pinnacle" earlier. Finally, in the context where the enigmatic crocodile also occurs, they seem to refer clearly to the skin of the creature, but with what effect it is difficult to say. An epithet for the holy but labyrinthine sea in "Then was my neophyte" is "the lane of scales." But none of these other uses, unfortunately, offers support for the possible reading that "Man was the scales . . . Tail, Nile and snout" identifies man with the crocodile, on the grounds that both are immortal.

III

It is clear that, in spite of its obscurities, "I, in my intricate image" illustrates the "complexity of controlled relations" which Howard Nemerov, in his review of the *Collected Poems*, admired in Thomas' complex style.[7] Nemerov's example, however, is "Hold hard, these ancient minutes in the cuckoo's month," a poem he describes as a "web of oneness" whose unity is fashioned through the skillful adjustment of a diversity of elements to one another. Thomas addresses a number of auditors in the poem, including the country and "the horns of England," but his message is directed chiefly to children. And it warns them that, in a universe of good and evil, they must be prepared, while they are experiencing joy, to encounter its opposite. The subject, according to Nemerov, is "The *fall* from nature into history, from the timeless to the organic." It warns of winter against the background of a summer landscape, drawing upon the two separate areas of the hunt and the amusements of children for its imagery. However, instead of following the obvious course of treating the hunt as the equivalent of autumn and the children's play as the equivalent of summer, and thus arriving at a poem built upon two sustained metaphors, Thomas borrows elements from the two fields indiscriminately to embody the various aspects of his subject: the duality of time as it is manifested in the alternation of the seasons.

In the first stanza, Time takes on the form of both horse and rider because these share the energy released in springtime; and the children are urged to hold fast to them. But in the last stanza, Time, whose effects change with the seasons, has become the menacing hound and the hawk. Though the children begin by accompanying the hunters, they are, in the end, the quarry, just as in life they are first the wards and finally the victims of Time. In the interest of pursuing this duality of his single vision, Thomas imposes a barren winter scene upon the summer landscape of the second stanza, as he warns the children to enjoy their games while they can. For, as the third stanza musically says, their countryside will soon be taken over, first by the huntsmen who signalize the end of summer, and then by a winter of primordial destructive energy which will attack both the "cuckoo's month" and the hunters themselves, "Crack like a spring in a vice, bone breaking April,/Spill the lank folly's hunter and the hard-held hope."

The children and the hunters, though generally antithetical, do have in common the fact that they use for their pleasure the landscape which winter takes from them. This parallel is subtly developed by means of "sport" and "game," ambiguous words equally appropriate to children and hunters, which have the effect of establishing criss-cross relationships between the two. "Your sport is summer" and "the summer's game" of the children contrast with the vigorous "sport" of the hunters and their beleaguered "game."

A number of the poem's details identify the hunt and the children's games with the changes of seasons. "The green blooms ride upward" is a key metaphor new in *Twenty-five Poems*, the identification of the movement of fertile energy with that of riding; hence when Time is personified as "a county man/ Over the vault of ridings," the phrase establishes two meanings through a pun. "The vault of ridings" is, literally, the horse's leap over some barrier, but it is also the tomb of summer growth, trod under by Time. The desolation of winter is suggested by the vision of the pools in December, presumably frozen, but "unskated"—not attracting the innocent and happy children. The representation of time as a hound running on the paws of the four seasons is impressive. And its horror is heightened by the fact that, since it has "a tail of blood," it is also the ghost of the fox which has been killed and had its brush taken; but it is still running, blended with its pursuer. The "harnessed valley" also links seasonal change to one of the poem's metaphors; it is harnessed as a horse is because its energies are controlled by the regulating alternation of seasons.

The metaphoric apparatus Thomas uses in "Hold hard" to wheel from one pole of meaning to another seems to resist his intentions, as though it were insufficiently saturated with the significance he attributes to it. By contrast, "Here in this spring," another poem on the ambiguity of the seasons, is far smoother; but it is also slighter. It asks a question without offering an answer, and it ends with the fatalistic conclusion implied by the worm, the slug, and the insect without trying to repair the rent made in the spiritual fabric by their appearance. "Here in this spring" is, in fact, incomplete. Its original draft contained some lines which have been omitted from the middle; but, more important, it concluded with a reply to the question at the end which represented a spiritual recovery and an assertion of continuing life. The lines are weak, and Thomas was wise to drop them, but the graceful poem that remains moves in the opposite direction from the one originally intended.

The first stanza of "Here in this spring" paradoxically draws three seasons together, exacting from each an image of desolation. The lines "Symbols are selected from the years'/Slow rounding of four seasons' coasts. . . ." explain that this procedure is being carried on without regard to chronology. From the trees and the sound of the cuckoo, Thomas continues, he would be inclined to adopt the hopeful mood of spring and summer; but the worms and the slug are truer indicators. Even more authoritative is the "timeless insect," which speaks of the annihilation toward which the world is moving. In the original draft this insect was merely a "summer bug"; it not only included in itself the ambiguities of summer and destruction but was also related to a midge which appeared in the rejected lines as a symbol of renewal. The insect in "Today, this insect" changes its form and becomes "a certain promise," but in this poem, whose optimistic ending has been truncated, the insect remains "the plague of fables," and it never undergoes the original hopeful metamorphosis.

The Bible was one of the very few literary influences Thomas was willing to acknowledge. He often made use of its stories to dramatize his own mysticism, absorbing them into the fabric of his rhetoric. "Before I knocked" and a number of allusions in the other poems of his first volume put the Christ story to this use, and in "Incarnate devil" in *Twenty-five Poems,* Thomas employs the legend of the Fall in a similar manner. The poem subjects the Biblical account of the events in the garden of Eden to a visionary critique, arguing that they implied deliverance. When Satan "stung awake" the "circle" of alternate sin and redemption, the fiddler God was present to give assurance that all would come to an ultimate harmony. The fresh universe of the second stanza is marked by moral duality; the newly minted, or "handmade" moon already bears on its divided face the darkness of sin and the light of forgiveness. The innocent Adam and Eve already know that the holiness of God is at hand in the most familiar natural events. As the poem concludes, heaven is present in the deepest darkness; and even the serpent, in spite of his intentions, plays an instrument that, in the fullness of time, becomes a part of the concord of creation.

"Incarnate devil" is an odd and charming collaboration of playfulness and mysticism. Thomas was capable of bringing some of the humor found in his essays and short stories into his poems on cosmic themes, and a similar contrast of tones occurs in "To-day, this insect." This poem begins by bringing sarcasm and self-criticism to bear on the use of religious legends found in "Incarnate devil." Thomas expresses the distrust of his medium of communication often felt by mystics, but he concludes with the reflection that Christ will appreciate his intentions. The first stanza appears to be a critical comment on his poetic method. The first line, though it seems to play no part in the syntax of the long sentence which forms the stanza, can be rationalized by the giant inversion of placing it after "made" in the seventh line. In short, it is "To-day, this insect, and the world I breathe" that have been made to witness the murder of the last line. This murder, it seems, is the mistreatment of the Eden legend. Self-mockingly reflecting that his poetry—"symbols"—has taken up both space and time, Thomas declares that he has "divided sense," as though with a guillotine. A clue to what he means by this is furnished by an early version of the poem, which suggests that Thomas felt he had been guilty of separating the intellectual and the spiritual.[8] There was a point in the development of his mysticism, we know, when the "two-framed globe" "spun into a score," and this stanza is another comment on the oversimplification which, Thomas feels, has led him to "murder" the Eden legend.

In the second stanza the poet reminds himself that, though it may be a foolish pious confection—"Winged like a sabbath ass this children's piece"—the Eden story has its serious spiritual value; for it presents Satan, who was already fully mature at the time of these events, and explains the fallen state of man—"blows Jericho on Eden." The subtly varied refrain about the insect is a fascinating puzzle. The insect does not disclose his significance readily; but, when he does, he helps us to the meaning of the poem. If we take the subject of the first two stanzas to be the process by which the Bible elevates ordinary tales into religious parables, it is possible to see the insect (which was, in the earlier version, a butterfly) as a symbol of this metamorphosis. The images of the shell and the chrysalis in the second stanza participate in this theme. Hence, the "insect fable" of the second refrain is a story that has imitated the insect's transformation; it has become a myth, embodying the "certain promise" of spiritual truth.

The final stanza, which widens the scope of this phenomenon, declares that all literature is endowed with spiritual values. The implication is that the fault the poet accused himself of in the first stanza is pardoned, for, in spite of its errors, his work will find acceptance as a part of the holy fabric of literature. The voice of Jesus, speaking the Greek of the New Testament, asserts the sacredness of secular tales; the "sweethearts" of all legends, he says, will share his martyrdom on the "tree of stories." Thus, all the creations of imaginative writers, the "fibs of vision"—including the idea of death, Hamlet, the windmill of Don Quixote, the Trojan Horse, the Lamb of God, and Job—are gathered into a single "cross of tales," a monument to the "madmen's love" of Jesus.

IV

Though Thomas was originally a poet of private cosmic vision, a time came when he began to focus upon his relations with other people and with external scenes and events as episodes in the drama of spiritual life. The change of poetic style which appears in *The Map of Love* (and becomes more pronounced in *Deaths and Entrances*) and the sustained lyricism of "In Country Sleep" involve not only a general surrender of the authority, intensity, and detachment of the seer but also a reversion to ordinary perplexities. These later poems still have cosmic reality as their background, but they are occupied with common emotions inappropriate to the visionary atmosphere of the earlier ones; they express sympathy, indignation, pride in human capacities, joy in nature, and love. Gradual clarifications of syntax and imagery accompany this shift in subject. As Thomas turns from the absolutely to the relatively incommunicable, accepting the familiar faces of experience instead of insisting upon the variety of forms it assumes in the fullness of time, his rhetoric becomes correspondingly simpler and more direct. Multiplicity of meaning is supplanted by richness of euphony. Instead of being diffused in an unpredictable manner through a dense fabric of metaphor and verbal ingenuity, meaning is controlled by a sparing and discriminating use of devices.

Thomas announced this change in "Once it was the colour of saying," which he described as a "Cwmdonkin poem" when he sent it to Watkins in a letter of December 29, 1938. When he was among the scenes of childhood described in the poem, a preoccupation with expression itself—"the colour of saying"—dominated his work, "Soaked my table." But the result of this obsession was that his subjects were "charmingly drowned" in "the seaslides of saying." He associates this kind of poetry with the cruelty of his gang of wandering boys, who mischievously threw stones at the couples they found making love in the shelter of the park's darkness. Such poetry was no more, he says, than "a lamp of lightning for the poor in the dark"—a blinding flash of no real use to humanity. And in the last two lines, he commits himself to a kind of poetry that will involve a sacrifice of his rhetorical powers: "Now my saying shall be my undoing." Instead of throwing a stone at the lovers, he will hold it as an embodiment of the simple and homely, in order to draw out the poetry latent in it. Anticipations of this shift also appear in *Twenty-five Poems* in "A grief ago," in "Grief, thief of time," and in "I have longed to move away." These are not markedly different in style from the mystic poems, but they do have in common a preoccupation with grief, a problem of life itself rather than life-and-death.

Though "Grief, thief of time" seems, as Tindall has observed, to be misleadingly punctuated, its general drift seems clear.[9] Grief is personified as a thief, "a knave of pain," because, in accordance with a principle formulated by Freud, memory tends to suppress what is painful. The major section of the first stanza is devoted to the argument that the old forget the glories of their youthful voyages because they involved hardships as well. The thief who dominates the second stanza is a compression of four figures found in a long, unpublished narrative poem written in September, 1933.[10] In this draft there are three thieves of light, sound and speech who rob the narrator of the respective senses, and a "thieving king" who appears to announce that loss of the senses amounts to death. In the manuscript poem, "Jack my father" is urged to allow the knaves to take away their loot in an injunction that means "Do not resist death."

But in "Grief, thief of time" these phrases have been worked into a passage that urges the poet's ancestors to let "the time-faced crook" set grief free, with its memories, from the prison of the grave. Thomas has not taken much trouble to distinguish the "crook" from the "thief," though they seem to be separate figures. The image of the thief is elaborated with consistency; he carries a "swag" and is not to be molested by the policemen's whistles. But the mixed metaphor of the bubbles with the bites of snakes seems both obscure and unsuccessful, and the four concluding lines do not seem well integrated with what has gone before. Still, the conclusion says that when grief, with its booty of memories has been resurrected, the "graveward gulf" that is, life, will be inhabited with traditions. Thus, the idea of the poem is a fairly conventional statement to the effect that the spirit flourishes in sorrow.

"I have longed to move away" is a poem wholly about daily life, without any touches of mysticism—a type Thomas succeeded with only in this instance, though "The Hand That Signed the Paper," "Paper and Sticks," and some of the later poems

might be classified with it. "I have longed to move away" is
a selection of passages from a longer poem drafted in March 1,
1933, which clearly shows that by "the spent lie" Thomas
meant no more than the conventional code of social life, sup-
porting E. Glyn Lewis' reading.[11] The poem, therefore, speaks
of the vanity of conventional social relationships; but it is saved
from easy cynicism by the suspicion that these customs may
contain truths and can be dangerous if they are ignored, and by
the conclusion that they deserve attention if only because they
are not worth the sacrifice of life, being "Half convention and
half lie." A single image—"death's feather"—related to Thomas'
mystic imagery appears oddly in the midst of a poem in which
he turns his back decisively, but only temporarily, on the cosmic
vision which is his usual subject in *Twenty-five Poems* as it was
in *18 Poems*.

CHAPTER 5

Later Poems

I

THE departures from Thomas' early manner which are barely perceptible in a number of the *Twenty-five Poems* dominate the poems in *The Map of Love*. "It is the sinner's dust-tongued bell" and "If my head hurt a hair's foot" are perhaps the only poems in this volume that fail to show Thomas shifting his ground. These later poems are usually written in response to some particular experience rather than to experience in general. Their points of departure are intimate and local rather than cosmic. The two poems on the self—"When all my five and country senses see" and "How shall my animal"—are occupied with specific insights, not with a mystic sense of identification with the universe. They exhibit interesting new tendencies toward acute self-analysis; a respect for the value of reportage; and, most significant of all, a suspicion of the inadequacy of mysticism. In these later poems, earthly things seem more immediate than visionary ones, and the discords of actuality prevail over the harmony of timelessness.

In turning to external subjects, Thomas was executing a complicated maneuver. He was setting aside the introspective basis of his mysticism without giving up mysticism itself, and acknowledging the relevance of the pathos to be found in the lives of others to his own spiritual experiences. He was also seeking confirmation for his convictions in the world outside himself. He could make effective use of such details borrowed from actuality as Ann Jones's stuffed fox, the "heron-priested shore," and the hunchback in the park eating his bread from a newspaper. But he showed little interest in developing in his poetry the objectivity found in his short stories. Instead, he invested such figures as lovers, children, and people recently

dead and such places as Laugharne and Sir John's Hill with his
own prior feelings, passionately appropriating them to the uses
of his spiritual drama. There is a sense in which this process
represents an extension rather than a renunciation of egotism.
But the confrontation of these subjects is nearly always accompanied by overtones of self-reproach; and the linkage Thomas
effects between his mysticism and the outer world is not used
to vindicate his visionary power but to reveal holiness in humble
people, landscapes, and animals.

These discoveries in the external world seem to have begun
with such subjective perceptions as those expressed in "When
all my five and country senses see."[1] The excellent control of
imagery and irony in this poem and the relatively limited range
of its allusions suggest a disposition on Thomas' part to explore
the specific insight fully instead of using it as a bridge to cosmic
truths. Unlike the early mystical poems which, Thomas admitted,
failed to develop their imagery fully within themselves, "When
all my five and country senses" fulfills a coherent program of
contrasts, antitheses, and ironies.

Its subject is a contrast between physical and intuitive love,
between the hedgehog of the heart and the foxes of the senses.
The best the bumpkin "country senses" can do is recognize the
limits of their capacity to evoke love, but the desire of the
aristocratic "noble heart" endures, even when the senses are
dead. The enumeration of the senses and their perceptive
powers involves a striking *dérèglement*, for it is the fingers
that "mark" (in the sense of seeing), the ears that "watch,"
the nostrils that "see." Yet this synesthetic disruption is not,
as it is in Symbolist doctrine, a path to absolute vision; for the
poem is ironically saying that even these exceptionally endowed
senses will learn nothing more than their inability to establish
communion with the beloved.

> The fingers will forget green thumbs and mark
> How, through the halfmoon's vegetable eye,
> Husk of young stars and handfull zodiac,
> Love in the frost is pared and wintered by. . . .

That is, fingers which are skillful enough in earthly gardens perceive, but cannot touch, the fertile powers represented in the moon and stars. "My nostrils see her breath burn like a bush"; that is, she is miraculous, but inaccessible. But the "witnesses" of the heart, less deliberate than the "spying senses," will fumblingly open themselves to love; the heart experiences desire, even when the "five eyes" of the senses are dead.

"How shall my animal" is another exploration of the self, but it is concerned, as Tindall's reading persuasively shows, with the problems of writing poetry, not with love.[2] The "animal" within the "skull" is Thomas' portion of the primordial creative energy of the cosmos. Capable of appearing in many forms, as the rich animal and plant imagery tells us, it appears in him as the poetic impulse. Far from celebrating his gift, however, Thomas laments his inability to do justice to it; it has come to him, he says, only to share his mortality. The poem thus repeats the familiar complaint of mystics and poets that words cannot communicate their visions.

The logic of the "animal" metaphor has as its basis the conviction that the force Thomas senses in himself is the same as the one he sees in the creatures of nature. It is irrational, uncontrollable, untameable, and irrelevant to such human concerns as poetry. The questions of the first two stanzas imply that the energy which would find free scope in nature is only imprisoned in him. Brought to life in such a shape as that of a stallion, says the second stanza, it would expend itself indiscriminately to "Love, labour and kill," producing the effects of birth, terror, and vitality appropriate to natural processes. Tindall has acutely interpreted the beginning of the third stanza as Thomas' contrast between poetasters and himself: others fish for artificial mermen, but he seeks the dangerous creature of his own intellectual depths, weaving his net of the poetic talents of "tongue and ear." But his attempts to tame it are useless; the "beast" can never be trained to delineate the "few seas" of terrestrial life, or to perform a trick of balance and precision with its horns. Instead, in the fourth stanza, it dies in the fisherman-poet's net. Among the images of destruction here, the familiar castrating scissors of Thomas' iconography appear, followed by the "wrackspiked maiden mouth" which similarly shears the inspiration of its glory. To communicate is to murder. Having come to expression, the original impulse loses its vitality.

It seems clear that in this poem the balance of fulfillment and destruction, which represents the visionary's destiny in many of the *18 Poems* and in "I, in my intricate image," has come down on the side of despair. Thomas once prayed for union with the creative power of the universe, and even believed he was achieving it, but he now sees that he can only betray it. A change in his view of the nature of language is also implied. Having once believed that words had the same pristine origin as any created thing, and the power of expressing fundamental truths:

> And from the cloudy bases of the breath
> The word flowed up, translating to the heart
> First characters of birth and death,

he now feels that the elemental energy is imprisoned behind the "spelling wall" of the intellect. This is, obviously, a poem of resignation; the visionary has recognized the limitations of the human condition, and he is testifying that even the remarkable creative power the poem itself employs is a debasement of the vitality of the cosmos.

"Twenty-four years" may be regarded as the last poem of the cosmic genre found in *18 Poems,* and the one in which Thomas takes leave of his early mysticism. Andrews Wanning, in his review of *The Map of Love,* points out that the poem admits, though it may not demand, a mystic interpretation.[3] He says that the imagery of the doorway and the tailor may serve equally well to represent the womb and the fetus, and "Death's Door" opening into the journey after death. "Dressed to die, the sensual strut begun" expresses "dying through living and living through dying"; as Wanning's observations show, the poem clearly makes use of the dialectic imagery of *18 Poems.* It speaks of death and life as if they were dovetailed into each other, for the tailor is at once the hunched fetus and the Atropos-like figure who bears the scissors used for severing the umbilical cord or the thread of life. In spite of the brave last line, "I advance for as long as forever is," (which was, as a matter of fact, borrowed for use here from a much earlier poem), the poem says that time is being irrevocably expended. The first line counts the years; the journey of life requires a shroud, the fulfillments of maturity mean only that the poet is "dressed to die." His veins are filled, not with immortal energy, but with the medium of worldly exchange that, once spent, is gone.

The key words of this brilliant fragment are "final" and "elementary." They suggest that once the scale has swung to the side of death, it will not be tipped back again. This is the view, not of a detached prophet scanning the cosmos as a whole, but of a mortal whose journey, though it may be part of a general balance, goes for him in a "final direction." The "forever" of the last line, Wanning suggests, is ironic; it is the "forever" of a single life. Thus, the element of renewal that gives the cosmos of *18 Poems* its symmetry is rejected; life is seen simply as a "sensual strut" toward death.

II

In the poems of Thomas' middle period, the lover, like the poet, is condemned to a fundamental betrayal. As a mystic poet, Thomas could treat sexual love as an embodiment of the creative energy of the universe, an earthly counterpart of mystic communion; but his own experiences taught him that human failings prepared hazards and torments for those who love. There is no lack of information about the external aspects of the relationship with his wife Caitlin, whose covert phases Thomas explores in such poems as "I make this in a warring absence" and as "Into her lying-down head." Augustus John has described the early days of their relationship.[4] What this romance had come to after some years of marriage is amply conveyed in Brinnin's accounts of his visits to the Thomas household in Laugharne and the disagreements between the two while they were in America.[5] Caitlin's book, *Leftover Life to Kill*, shows that she was driven by grotesquely irrational forces in her feelings toward Thomas. These reports give the impression that their relationship was like the one in *Wuthering Heights*: full of intolerable resentments but, nevertheless, both natural and indispensable to them.

Later Poems

The lovers who are seen from a distance in Thomas' poems, such as the ones stoned in the park by the mischievous boys of "Once it was the colour of saying," and those to whom his poems are dedicated in "In my craft or sullen art," are innocent, troubled, and the objects of tender veneration. But, when he speaks of his own love affairs, Thomas shows that he has experienced hostility and resentment. For example, the enigmatic "Not from this anger," as is clearly shown by the stumbling draft written in April, 1933,[6] is about a painful moment when the poet's sweetheart, having been rejected by another man, spitefully rejects the poet in turn. The anger is hers, and the refusal is something she has suffered. As a result, reflects the poet, there is no hope for him. The sky sags and the sun leaves its path, for "not from this anger" can he expect love for him to emerge.

The prose sense of "I make this in a warring absence" is a chronicle of spiteful rivalry. Deserted by Caitlin for reasons of "pride," Thomas experiences a complex of feelings that include nothing more profound than remorse, self-righteousness, and erotic desire. He releases his feelings toward her in an orgy of hostility which leads to self-reproach, to the recovery of a sense of proportion, and finally to a reconciliation, undertaken with the full knowledge that future conflicts are likely. The poem, written a few months after his marriage, was apparently in commemoration of an actual quarrel and separation, for it was originally called "Poem to Caitlin." Thomas attributed considerable importance to this poem, for, when he sent it to Vernon Watkins on November 13, 1937, he said that he had spent "weeks" in writing it. During that time he seems to have sent his jangled feelings on a long tour of his world of imagery, so that they returned clothed in a complex and characteristic rhetoric.

A large number of the tropes in the poem are generated from comparisons with elements of the sea and sky. These fan out over a wide range of complexity. "Like an approaching wave I sprawl to ruin" is at once one of the best and most conventional of Thomas' single images. But it is only a part of a chain of sea-images which rival his most ingenious metaphoric constructions, such as the "roped sea-hymen" of the second stanza, apparently intended to represent capture and violation. The closing passages of the poem offer an example of Thomas' trick of spinning the gold of poetry out of the straw of cliché. The basis of the "cloud of pride" image in the stanza before the last is, of course, the association of the cloud with the trouble Caitlin has caused. The cloud, pursues the final stanza, has quiet expanses, representative of reconciliation; but Thomas can see from Caitlin's glance that she is storing up resentments for some new disagreement. Hence, ". . . my love pulls the pale, nippled air,/Prides of to-morrow suckling in her eyes," and the cloud is transformed, for the purpose of this idea, into breasts that pacify, but also nourish destructive energies.

This is the last of a series of metaphoric transformations through which Caitlin's crucial "pride" passes. At first a feeling more sympathetic to Thomas—a pride, perhaps, in him or his poetry—it appears as a fusion of ship, fountain, and tree, all things that stand proudly forth, reaching to heaven through earthly structures and "this weak house," Thomas himself. But this pride, says the second half of the long opening sentence, is now bedraggled and cast aside, a child in a child's world.

The poet begins to assign images to his own feelings in the third stanza; the nettle and the pigeon convey the statement that Caitlin's absence arouses feelings of both innocence and guilt, but it is the innocence that is painful, the guilt that is soothing. The details that follow—the virgin's shell, the pearls, the mermaid in the cavern—nearly all related to the sea, present Caitlin as various objects of desire. "Omens" is oddly used as a verb; it is Caitlin who "omens/Whalebed and bulldance," symbols of powerful erotic desire. Having tried to "follow" her (that is, presumably, to secure agreement) and failed, Thomas, in a passage that seems for the first time since the opening of the poem to descend to a literal level, walks the beach, rebelling against the nature of things and abandoning himself to horrible fantasies of revenge upon Caitlin, in which "I" "Storm her sped heart, hang with beheaded veins/Its wringing shell, and let her eyelids fasten."

But this violence brings remorse; a sudden awareness of his errors closes round him like a pyramid, transforming him into a mummy. He is a "hero" only ironically, for the "anatomist" from the surface, who examines his remains, like an archaeologist, with a "sun-gloved hand," finds no nobility. Instead, the other mummies cry out reproaches through their "inchtaped lips." The last two stanzas narrate a widening of Thomas' sense of the universe in which the lovers' quarrel has taken place, a new perceptiveness that leads to the establishment of a "forgiving presence."

When he sent this poem to Watkins, Thomas expressed dissatisfaction with the fourth and fifth lines of the last stanza as being "too fluent," providing, in his comments on them, one of his few glosses on his verse. The lines are: "A calm wind blows that raised the trees like hair/Once where the soft snow's blood was turned to ice." Thomas' explanation of these lines is: "Once upon a time, before my death and resurrection, before the 'terrible' world had shown itself to me (however lyingly, as lines 6 and 7 of the last verse might indicate) as not so terrible after all, a wind had blown that had frightened everything and created the first ice and the first frost by frightening the falling snow so much that the blood of each flake froze."[7] This sentence shows that Thomas could relate his spiritual development to the world's earliest events. But the benign cosmos of his early vision is now suspected to be false, as the parenthesis says. It also shows that the obscure image is based on the linking of a naïve personification with a naïve cliché in "the blood of each flake froze."

In this poem, Thomas applies the style of his early mystic period to a transient emotional episode. An extreme rhetoric, adapted to the requirements of extreme spiritual situations, is put at the disposal of a circumscribed subject. Thomas is obviously trying to emphasize the larger implications of the emotions aroused in the lovers' quarrel, and he succeeds to some extent in the stanzas describing his hostility and his despair (stanzas three to six). But the feelings evoked by his disagreement with Caitlin seem to diminish rather than enlarge the scope of his vision. The rhetorical effects belonging to cosmic awareness do not seem to arise naturally from the subject; they have the effect of ornamental additions. As a result of this disproportion, the poem is embarrassed by a profusion and ingenuity inappropriate to the lyric cry.

"Into her lying down head" is another but less personal complaint about the contradictions of love. In sending this poem (before rewriting the last ten lines and making other revisions) to Vernon Watkins, Thomas called it "a poem about modern love." He quoted the note he had written about it:

All over the world love is being betrayed as always, and a million years have not calmed the uncalculated ferocity of each betrayal or the terrible loneliness afterwards. Man is denying his partner man or woman and whores with the whole night, begetting a monstrous brood; one day the brood will not die when the day comes but will hang on to the breast and the parts and squeeze his partner out of bed. Or, as a title, One Married Pair.[8]

Thomas is saying in the poem that physical love is experienced as a general rather than as a personal communion, that the lovers are prevented from reaching each other, and that it is therefore transformed into an exercise of lust. In the first stanza the woman's mind is possessed, not by thoughts of the man who is making love to her, but by a host of rival lovers—mythical, fictional, and historical. In the second her husband is displaced by an "always anonymous beast," a lustful figure of her imagination. This isolation of the lovers from each other is seen, in the last stanza, as a part of the order of nature; their hostility and frustration, a "libidinous betrayal," is reflected in the sand and shells of the shore, in the peril of the she bird who is prey to the hawk, and in the isolated blade of grass and the stone. The last part of this stanza recapitulates the situation; the woman is isolated between "two wars": that of her disturbed husband with himself, and that of her turbulent erotic imagination from which arise "the second comers, the severers" who are the partners of her lust.

The poem's point of origin in Thomas' feelings was no doubt a disturbing complex of Puritanism, jealousy, and self-pity at the inadequacy of his relations with his wife. One of its features preserves the dangerous irrationality of this state of mind: the attribution of passions and motives to the imaginary rival lovers makes them hallucinatory figures. But, with regard to the rest, it is notable how far Thomas has been able to carry his subject from the vindictive feelings in which it must have originated. He told Watkins that he had never worked harder on a poem; he

succeeded in transforming the psychic adultery which he so
bitterly resented into one of the realities of the human condition,
attended by both glory and sorrow. The imaginary loves the
woman enjoys are heralded by Noah's dove, but the deliverance
it announces is an ambiguous one. In moving through the realm
of erotic tradition, the woman is linked with irresistible and fundamental forces,

> Last night in a raping wave
> Whales unreined from the green grave
> In fountains of origin gave up their love,

and justice is certainly being done to the beauty of her experience in the remarkable

> Man was the burning England she was sleep-walking, and
> the enamouring island
> Made her limbs blind by luminous charms. . . .

These passages recall the union of the girl and the sun-god in
"The Marriage of a Virgin."

Thomas will not insist that the retribution of the second
stanza, the arrival of the phallic monster who dominates the
wife's imagination, is wholly painful for her. The pain is suffered by the husband, who is exiled from these "holy unholy"
joys; and the notion that his wife complains of "the theft of
the heart" is his. But the final stanza testifies most convincingly
to Thomas' capacity for submerging his resentments by withholding blame and for seeing the wife's infidelity of spirit as
a fact of nature. The dreaming woman is like the unsuspecting
she-bird who invites the hawk, and she is finally depicted as
lying "innocent" between two dark and active forces. It is fair
to conclude that the rhetorical elaboration of this poem succeeds where that of "I make this in a warring absence" fails;
it transmutes personal resentments whose straightforward expression could not be of any literary value into a balanced,
perceptive testimonial to the impossibility of the perfect union
lovers desire.

Although two of the poems in *The Map of Love*—"If my head
hurt a hair's foot" and "A saint about to fall"—are reversions

to a theme typical of *18 Poems* (an unborn child surveying his destiny), they were written, not as general observations, but in response to the birth of Thomas' first child, Llewelyn, in February, 1939. "If my head hurt a hair's foot," written in March, 1939, is one of the later poems that continues the style of *18 Poems;* birth and death operate within the poem as two magnetic poles, drawing the imagery to themselves and occasionally fusing them in a single self-contradictory image, such as "worm of the ropes." However, the poem is somewhat less complicated in syntax and metaphor than most of the earlier poems, and it has a realistic moment not at all typical of them. In this dialogue with its mother, the embryo offers to forgo entering the "clouted scene" of the discordant household, and adding to its problems. (His speech does not profit much from the prevalence of "game phrases" reflecting children's pursuits— the "unpricked ball," "bubbles," "bully," and so on.) The mother answers to the effect that "Men must endure/ . . . their coming hither." The child is condemned to live. He will be trapped between "The grave and my calm body," and must "Rest beyond choice" in the dubious interval of life.[9]

In "A saint about to fall," the balancing of Thomas' early mysticism with a realism inspired by poverty and threats of war progresses further. (However, this poem was written before "If my head hurt a hair's foot.") The child will enter the world, asserts the poet, as "a saint," an actor in the cosmic drama; but he will find only prospects of suffering and violence, which are conveyed in mundane imagery of slum life. The child, in descending from heaven, is ironically met in mid-air by a rubble of shattered religious articles rising from the impact of a bomb on the city. This annihilation of naïve faith is summarized in one of Thomas' greatest and simplest lines, "Glory cracked like a flea." A series of apostrophes expressing the expectation that the holy child will miraculously transform reality sketches the squalor, suffering, and threat of bloodshed to which he is being born. The hope of miracle does not prevent the intrusion of sordid particulars into the usual dignity of Thomas' rhetoric. "The old mud hatch" on "the crotch of the squawking shores" is Thomas' cynical realism about the house which is to be the child's home, and the importance of domes-

tic squalor as an element in human suffering is effectively fixed
in the "dishrag hands" and "the pressed sponge of the forehead."
Even poverty finds its way into the poem in the disastrous
"agony has another mouth to feed." These are slow sufferings;
more dramatic ones are threatened by war, by the "herods"
bearing murderous steel, by the moment when hostilities will
begin, signaled both by the small detail of the soldier's thumb
pressing the safety-catch on his weapon and by the large fact
of the sun's position. These will turn the child's country into a
"thundering bullring" of violence. Though Thomas is calling
upon the child through most of the poem to bring deliverance
from these threats, the threats carry far more conviction than
the prayer. The poem is a restatement, in effect, of "Before
I knocked," with emphasis shifted from the redemption of spiritual life to the horrors of earthly reality.

III

In approaching ultimate realities through personal experiences of grief and love, as he does in "I make this in a warring
absence" and in the two poems about the birth of Llewelyn,
Thomas begins the descent to earthly subjects found in "After
the Funeral," in most of the poems of *Deaths and Entrances,*
and in his later work generally. The balance and continuity of
the universal processes open to the poet's vision in the early
poems justify, perhaps, a certain indifference toward individual
suffering. But as he turns, in a familiar Wordsworthian shift,
from the introspective imagination of youth to encounters
with people and external nature, visible realities rival cosmic
vision as sources of truth. Ordinary events, humble folk, and
local scenery, together with the compassion and tenderness
these things evoke, occupy the foreground of these poems. They
are about those "Who pay no praise or wages/Nor heed my
craft or art."

In the later poems, the figures and landscapes have a new
solidity, a new self-sufficiency, and the dialectic vision no longer
penetrates them as though they were no more than windows
opening on a timeless universe. Nevertheless, the poetic imagination is present to reach beyond immediate feelings and to

establish relationships between immediate and fundamental realities. For Thomas, as for Wordsworth, the memory of mysticism could operate, when mysticism itself failed, to suggest the poetry of the visible earth. But his resemblance to Wordsworth must not be exaggerated. For Thomas, nature is only the most obvious manifestation of cosmic conflicts that are foreign to Wordsworth's philosophy. Wordsworth finds moral strength in nature because it is the handiwork of a benign divinity; Thomas finds moral strength in it only because it exhibits evil and good as parts of a single design, and therefore offers an opportunity for coming to terms with the austere realities of existence.

One of the favorite subjects of Thomas' stories and later poems—a Wordsworthian one, as it happens—is the figure of the natural, lunatic, or simpleton, (often a woman) who offers love or devotion to an uncomprehending world but who meets with suffering or indifference. Two poems about the deaths of humble and virtuous women, "The tombstone told when she died" and "After the Funeral," illustrate his treatment of this theme. A short early draft of "The tombstone told when she died" makes it clear that the woman is a virgin only in the sense that she married a man she did not love.[10] Expecting a child, she fled to "a stranger's bed," went mad, and died before her child was born. Thomas' method with subjects taken from life is well represented in this example. The style is, for Thomas, unusually bare and reportorial; but it is appropriate to a subject that has its own eloquence. And it demonstrates that the passionate, abundant lyricist of *18 Poems* is also capable of a sensitive, discriminating simplicity. The poem does not record the person, but more particularly, the poet's reaction to her; it is not an act of empathy but an enfolding of the woman into Thomas' thoughts, "a hurried film" of consciousness.

In "After the Funeral," Thomas arrives at a full mastery of the intimate, without surrendering the insights available to mystic vision. The poem is, in fact, a dialogue which arrives at a working agreement between the realistic and the cosmic imaginations. After the opening review of the details of the burial and the parenthetical admission that Ann herself would consider Thomas' praise exaggerated, six lines in a magniloquent style appropriate to "Ann's bard" call upon the countryside to bear witness to her virtue. This ritualistic celebration renders her a "skyward statue." Nevertheless, pursues Thomas, his monumental notion of her is based upon the truth of her hard life, and it enables him, as the last two lines of the poem state, to see how even the pathetic ornaments of her dingy parlor reflect universal Love.

The nearly literal cataloging of the physical details of the funeral creates its poetic effect through subtle displacements of word order and sense. The expression "mule praises, brays" begins the rhetorical process of the poem—the transformation of homely actuality into material for a rite of celebration. In accordance with the traditional pattern of the elegy, the physical and specific melt into the spiritual and universal, as Thomas, having returned to visit the dead woman's house years after the funeral, recalls how her kindness filled his child's world. The parenthesis is significant as an acknowledgment that this praise of Ann is an *ex parte* view and does not square with other possible attitudes. There is a matter-of-fact awareness here, as there is not in the early mystic poems, that cosmic vision is not necessarily final, that alternative readings of experience exist, and that life may end in modesty, resignation, and silence.

The six lines in bardic style are a deliberate exercise in pantheism, corresponding with the apotheosizing process of the traditional elegy, a self-conscious transfiguration of the simple woman and the plain country scene into a deity inhabiting her haunts. The incisively-observed physical details that follow do not undercut, but support the effect of this display of poetic artifice. Thomas is working out a balance of the homely and the exalted, a ground for maintaining that both are necessary. Although he has fully admitted the feebleminded old country wife with her earth-bound virtues into his cosmos, she does not displace the visionary adolescent who has been Thomas' chief spokesman in his poems. Both the mute, unconscious beauty of the woman and the soaring imagination of her interpreter are necessary to the resolution of the last two lines. Only the "monumental/Argument" of the pantheistic rhetoric can bring forth the implications of the fox's lung and the fern.

"On the Marriage of a Virgin" is another poem about a woman who moves between the realm of legend and the mortal world. As a virgin, she is married to nature and shares its sacramental powers; her sacredness, as John L. Sweeney has pointed out, is expressed through pagan and Christian images of love and miracle.[11] The Danaë-like image of the second stanza describes her possession by a divinity; the precarious suggestion that the sun had at one time come to stay with her, raising his "luggage" to her eyes as she awoke, pursues the same idea. But, in the last two lines she has exchanged this communion for ordinary mortal life; she has found in physical desire a compulsion as powerful as that of external nature.

Two early drafts of "On the Marriage of a Virgin" offer an opportunity to trace its development from a very different original. First drafted, according to Thomas' dating, on March 22, 1933, it was revised in January, 1941, and then rewritten in the summer of 1941 before being published in *Life and Letters Today* in October. The first draft laments the girl's marriage on the ground that she has exchanged the love of the sun which touched her pillow in the morning for that of a husband who does not love her and whom she cannot love. A prosaic final stanza states that the marriage can be interpreted either as a sacrifice or as the deterioration of "sun love to man." The second version, written nearly eight years later, is not radically different from the first; but Thomas did succeed, through heavy corrections, in improving some of the imagery and vocabulary. One of the working titles of the second draft, "Dog-in-a-Manger," suggests not only that the poem was about a girl Thomas himself had loved, but that he also realized, when he applied this title to it, that it had been inspired by jealousy.

Both of the early drafts are in irregular tetrameter lines, and they create an effect entirely unlike the richness, complexity, and swimming smoothness of the published poem. They also emphasize the inadequacy of the husband, a subject hardly touched by the final version. The increased animation and resonance of the final version reflect a change in the poet's attitude toward his subject. The two early drafts attribute no religious significance to the girl's virginity and do not make use of the Christian symbolism in the first stanza. The marriage openly lamented in the early drafts is approved in the final version. The original form of the final line describes the husband's love as inferior; but in the final poem it has become "that other sun," and is described as "the jealous coursing of the unrivalled blood." It is clear that a poem originally written to complain of the loss of a sweetheart has been transformed into a declaration that divine love may be fittingly sacrificed for mortal love. It asserts, in fact, that the bright love of the composite deity which the virgin has given up has its dark counterpart in the nocturnal love of human beings.

"The Conversation of Prayer" is one of Thomas' most consummately controlled performances in the blending of antithetical elements; it suffuses transitional moments in two ordinary lives with spiritual dignity, and subjects the grandeur of cosmic vision to the control of a cool and witty dexterity. The fancy that the destinies of the praying child and of the man ascending the stairway are interchangeable assumes that the universe is a spiritual unity in which each part shares the glory and suffering of all. It should be noted that the reversal of lots predicted by the poem does not raise a question of moral judgment. The sincerity of the man who prays for his sweetheart's life and the indifference of the child saying his routine prayers are not the results of individual choice; they are contrasting manifestations of the same divinity, which acts through them, using them as its innocent agents. The exchange is neither reward nor punishment; the reversed situation is, after all, no more terrible or joyous than the original one, but exactly equivalent. Between such alternative distributions of joy and suffering the poem envisions a steady balance which reflects the neutral, austere justice of the universal process.

The pathos and irony of this criss-crossing of fates is supported by a phonic and rhetorical structure of remarkable design.[12] In an intricate system of inner rhymes and assonances, the word in the middle of each line rhymes with the terminal word of the line before or after it; and the middle and final words of the last line of each stanza rhyme with the corresponding words in the first. (The last line varies this structure.) The subtle pattern that results very effectively weaves the poem into a single musical unit. The idea that the situations of the man and the child are reciprocal is wittily reflected in a system of verbal ambiguities; the separate prayers, unknown to the speakers, constitute a "conversation," an interchange, which not only "turns" or reverses its import as it rises to the sky but "turns on the quick and the dead," depends on situations involving the living and dead, and also subjects them to surprise attack. One of the most striking features about the poem is its sparing use of imagery; the local images are nearly all ineffective. The poem does its work through a series of semantic and syntactic balances that develop its antithetical structure and also through its subtle, flowing music.

"A Refusal to Mourn," which uses visionary insights to transmute common feelings, is likely to remain one of the permanent poems of the English language. The commanding presence in the poem is that of the child; but Thomas renders her a representative of the inescapable fate of humanity and justifies the "refusal" the poem articulates by placing her death within the framework of the universal process. The first three lines of the poem contain a celebrated compound adjective, modifying "darkness," which makes explicit the death and renewal of the natural cycle:

> Never until the mankind making
> Bird beast and flower
> Fathering and all humbling darkness. . . .

The signatures of Thomas' universe are found in the "harness" that controls the sea, in the "grains" of elemental life that receive the child's body, and in the metaphor of "riding," expressing the movement and energy of the river. The "darkness" is, of course, the poet's death, which he anticipates as a re-entry into the vitality of the earth. Since the child has undertaken a similar journey back to the community of the dead and to natural origins, mourning is not called for. But this view earns its validity only by first fully acknowledging the appropriateness of grief as a reaction to the death of the child.

The poem cannot be described as a paradoxical denial on Thomas' part that he will not do what he is doing. He says he will not mourn, and he does not mourn, giving sufficient reasons for refraining. There is, however, a subtle paradox in his adoption of a ritualistic tone and religious imagery to argue that formal observation of the child's death would be an impertinence. The effect of the metaphors involving traditional religious symbols is, on the one hand, to suffuse the elements of nature with "sacredness" and, on the other, to imply that the recognized religions are only provisional forms of the permanent holiness of nature. The merely historical "Zion," the archaic "synagogue," and the tradition of the "stations" of the cross are all limited human inventions; but they are given a new authenticity when they are linked with the concrete, familiar, and primordial elements of water, corn, and breath. The holy symbols stand within the greater holiness of the cosmos; the sacredness which is primary and intrinsic in the water is secondary and arbitrary with regard to Zion. To lament the child's death formally would be to invoke the lesser sacredness rather than the greater and thereby to "blaspheme down the stations of her breath."

The general effect of the poem is, in fact, a resolution of contraries, a working out of the opposition between the pathetic event of the child's death and an austere recognition of universal process, between rites consecrated by human agreement and the elements of nature. The perfect ambiguity of the final line brings this unity of opposites to a focus. "After the first death, there is no other" means both that death is final and that it is followed by immortality. The simplicity of this formulation seems intended to defy resolution; it does not mean one or the other but both. Like the poem itself, it evokes compassion for human suffering and acceptance of the greater reality within which this suffering occurs. If the two attitudes are contradictory, "We must," as G. S. Fraser says in his comment on this line, "respect the baffling simplicity of Thomas' unitary response and not impose abstract categories on him."[13]

If "A Refusal to Mourn" shows a certain indifference to the child's suffering in its emphasis upon her symbolic value, the related "Ceremony After a Fire Raid" is far more vulnerable to this objection. The resignation of the earlier poem is developed from a mediation among three incommensurate attitudes: humanitarian indignation, rejection of conventional mourning, and acceptance of the natural cycle which enables the poet to

see the child's death as a representative experience and a return
to her origins. "Ceremony After a Fire Raid" quickly bypasses
the dead baby, its subject, to move to an ornate and ringing
assertion of piety. In this way, it foregoes both the conflict of
beliefs and the irony found in the earlier poem. After its grotesque presentation in the first stanza, the terrible fate of the
child is treated as a sacramental occasion whose human significance is occluded by the divine necessities it illustrates.[14]

Thomas' short story, "The Burning Baby," which shares its
odd subject with the poem and has a number of other parallels
to it as well, suggests that Thomas was deeply engaged by the
sacramental overtones of a child's death by fire, as if he felt
that an episode of such ultimate horror must have sacred significance. In the story, the burning of the baby is a rite performed by its father with the intention of expurgating the incestuous relationship from which it sprang. The death of the child
in the poem, though it is an accident of war, is seen as a
similar rite, for an expiatory element is attached to it in the
third stanza. The child's death appears, not as an episode in
the life of humanity, but as a spiritual instance. The poem
is, in fact, not a lyric, but a "ceremony." It does not attempt
the hard work of coining convictions from experience but offers
a ritualistic rehearsal of established articles of faith. This quality
is emphasized, of course, by its magnificent music, by its
excellent organization, and by the technical facility displayed
in it. Its rhetoric is oriented away from the pathetic subject,
and toward a general vision richly shot with legend and ceremonial, and presented with a factitious baroque energy. There is
vigor and paradox but little genuine feeling or irony in the
representation of the ultimate spiritual deliverance as a time
when

> ... the blood shall spurt,
> And the dust shall sing like a bird
> As the grains blow, as your death grows, through our heart.

The three parts of the poem are so distinct that no estimate
will apply equally well to all of them. In the carefully fashioned
stanzas of the first section, the assertions of the long lines seem
to spring from the tight, repetitive bases of the short ones pre-

ceding them. The first four stanzas describe the effect the child's death has upon the city's populace; the immediate horror calls their attention to the ultimate framework of the beginning and ending within which it has its place. The last line of this section, "Seed of sons in the loin of the black husk left," mourns the child on the rather abstract ground that it has been cut off from taking part in the procreative energies of nature. The more loosely organized, wandering lines of the second section lament that the child has been denied the spiritual awareness of the Judeo-Christian tradition.

The final section, which makes only a passing allusion to the child and is different enough from the rest to stand as a separate poem, calls upon the "fountain" of divine energy to flood the symbols of worship found in both human religious institutions and in the elements of nature. This section carries a conviction lacking in the others, perhaps because it is a restatement of the visionary truths of *18 Poems*. The cathedrals, weathercocks, and clock of the first few lines are symbols of man-made religion; the sun, bread, and wine of the lines following represent the holiness innate in nature. These sequences of images, like the images of "A refusal to mourn," establish a relation between the smaller worship and the greater one. All of these symbols, from the "luminous cathedrals" to "the wine burning like brandy," share the light of the holy fire that has consumed the child. The thought of "Over the whirling ditch of daybreak/Over the sun's hovel and the slum of fire. . . ." is the same as that in "the stained flats of heaven" from "A saint about to fall," a feeling that the sordidness of the war has invaded nature.

As in "A saint about to fall" and in "A Refusal to Mourn," however, the poem envisions a flood of spiritual deliverance arising from the destruction of war. But in the incoherent fervor of "Glory glory glory," Thomas has left behind both the shrewd skepticism of "Glory cracked like a flea" and the passionate sympathy felt in "A Refusal to Mourn." The spiritual victory of the poem, encountering too little resistance, is too easily won; it is gorgeous and magnificently controlled, as any ceremony can be, but it moves, like a ceremony, among symbols divorced from their sources of value.

In "Among those killed in the dawn raid was a man aged a

hundred," it is the age rather than the youth of the victim that leads Thomas to consider him against the background of the cosmic cycle. As in "A Refusal to Mourn," the common rites are disapproved on the ground that they would desecrate. The imagery of locks, keys, and chains makes the point that the man's long life was an imprisonment and his death a release: ". . . the keys shot from their locks and rang." His long servitude has made him an essential part of the natural order, "The morning is flying on the wings of his age," and the storks, one for each of his years, appear to celebrate it. Having thus passed into the fabric of nature in a pagan apotheosis, he has no need of the "common cart" of the passage into a formalized Christian heaven.

Thomas' sympathy is aroused not only by the helpless who die but by the helpless who live. Madmen, in particular, figure in his poems and stories as counterparts of the visionary, for they share both his freedom from immediate reality and the penalty of exile. In Thomas' treatment of deranged people there are both the traditional romantic respect for irrational ideas and Dostoevski's worship of the holiness of idiocy. Two themes related to this subject which receive fuller development in some of the stories appear in the poem "The Hunchback in the Park." The hunchback, in turning from the persecutions of the boys to a mistress fashioned by his imagination, finds in private reality the solace denied him by actuality. Further, the imagination, after its retreat, wheels about to impose its power on the visible world, exercising the "omnipotence of thought" which Freud describes as the consequence of unbridled narcissism. Hence, the park and its features become, like Alice in the White King's dream, creations of the hunchback's thoughts; according to the rhetoric of the poem, the trees and water enter when the park is unlocked and the hunchback comes; and, when he goes home, all is "unmade" and follows him out. Only his dream woman is left behind as testimonial to the dominance of imagination over actuality. The actuality in the poem is supplied by the child who is the speaker, and whose naïve reports about the appearance of the hunchback and his surroundings provide the necessary background for the imaginative assertion.

When the hunchback rolls up the scroll of the park and takes it home in his thoughts, the boys who are his enemies are included, and they remain "innocent as strawberries"; for, as G. S. Fraser has effectively explained, the universe, as Thomas and the hunchback conceive it, is a single brotherhood. "Hunter and hunted; mocked and mocker; boys and hunchback; growth and decay; life and death; dream and reality; all sets of polar opposites are, for Thomas, at some level equally holy and necessary; holy is the hawk, holy the dove. . . ."[15] The level to which Fraser refers is that of the absolute vision found in Thomas' earlier poems; in "The Hunchback" it is approached through the material world.

"Love in the Asylum" may be considered a sequel to "The Hunchback in the Park," for the speaker is just such a natural as the hunchback, and the girl is an imaginary mistress, like the figure in the hunchback's mind. The themes of the comforting power of imagination and the omnipotence of thought recur. The dream woman is a mad girl, and she brings to her lover, who has been unable to find love in the real world, a dispensation which is "delusive"; but this does not prevent her from barring the door against the night, flooding the madhouse with light, and taking the dreamer in a cosmic, primeval embrace. Since the asylum is "heaven-proof," the madman seeks deliverance in the compassion offered by irrationality, in order to unite with fundamental creation, to "Suffer the first vision that set fire to the stars." The madman in search of love is a significant figure in Thomas' mind; he appears in "The Tree," in "The Dress," and in "The Vest"; The Mouse and the Woman" is a story that amounts to a prose version of "Love in the Asylum."

CHAPTER 6

Last Poems

I

IN the summer of 1951 Thomas told John Malcolm Brinnin that
he had decided to write only happy poems. But he added that
they were to be "poems in praise of God's world by a man who
doesn't believe in God," and he said that he found it harder
to write happy poems that were plausible than tragic ones. The
four important and distinctive odes—"Poem in October," "Fern
Hill," "Over Sir John's hill," and "Poem on His Birthday"—are
no doubt the results of this determination. They are all poems
of praise. They praise nature, life, and sensation itself. But
the sense of "doom in the bulb" which forms a part of the symmetry of nature in the earlier poems is not left entirely behind.
The difference is that it is outweighed by the joy which flows
into the four odes from the experiences of nature they celebrate. Knowledge of death and of suffering is now only a temporary stage on the road to a wider awareness, a joyous acceptance of existence and an ecstatic immersion in the vitality
of the universe.

In style, these poems represent a decisive change. The superb
control Thomas always maintains over sound is put to a new
use in them. The early poems depend for the hermetic effects
they achieve on consonantal correspondences, tightly organized
verbal constructions, subtle off-rhymes, and obsessively repeated short rhythmic patterns. The music of these later poems is
far less measured and restrained. Its sound is characterized less
by consonants than by resonant, even orotund vowels; the rhythms are not tight and repetitive, but loose, flowing, and brilliantly contrasted. The syntax is correspondingly more conventional and less insistently economical, with a freer use of articles
and connectives. This is the style that appears in many of the

poems written after 1944, including "In Country Sleep," "A Winter's Tale," "In the White Giant's Thigh," and the "Author's Prologue" to the *Collected Poems*.

The four odes are not uniform in style, but they lend themselves to a number of generalizations.[1] Their imagery is far more accessible than that of the earlier poetry. Though an occasional allusion to the specialized associations that govern the imagery of *18 Poems* and *Twenty-five Poems* occurs, their rhetoric is in general derived from conventional sources. They are inspired by some event or occasion—two of them are birthday poems—and are closely in touch with a visible subject or particular scenes. Further, the imagery is suffused with the atmosphere and animal life of these places, making abundant use of their shells, birds, fish, and forests. These landscapes are the settings of a Wordsworthian moral drama played out between the vision and innocence of youth and the faltering imagination and accumulated knowledge of age.

"Poem in October" is, in fact, essentially a recapitulation of "Tintern Abbey." Through an experience with a familiar landscape, the mature man secures a momentary access to the lost imaginative powers of childhood, and what he remembers infiltrates the present moment with a joyful though obscure sense of order. Appearing among the first poems of *Death and Entrances*, which share its comparatively conventional syntax and freedom from congestion, "Poem in October" broaches a number of propositions new in Thomas' poetry. It shows a new willingness to commit rhetoric to the purposes of description; no mystic overtones are felt in the "sea wet church the size of a snail" or in the other picturesque details of the walk and the view. There is a mellowed disposition to seek epithets innocent of cosmic implications and useful for ornament alone, such as "a springful of larks" and "fond climates." The music, of course, is new; and the notion that the spectacle of nature inspires joy, as the exuberant conclusion states, is foreign to the tormented dialectic of Thomas' earlier poems.

Nevertheless, at least three of Thomas' visionary convictions survive in "Poem in October" to establish its continuity with *18 Poems*. It celebrates the relationship between nature and the self; it attributes to nature the capacities of language; and it proclaims nature's holiness. The poem is ostensibly devoted to a trivial but ardent assertion that the world belongs to the poet alone on his birthday. The morning town speaks to him with a special intimacy; the birds spell his name in the sky; and in the central experience of the poem, the landscape of his recollection is skillfully dovetailed with his shame and joy, so that it seems continuous with himself and capable of sharing his feelings. The poem is a reading of nature, whose meaningfulness is suggested in such imagery as "parables of sunlight/And the legends of the green chapels," and in the fancy of the birds forming the poet's name. The same images speak of the holiness of nature, as does the celebrated "heron-priested shore." But this devotion contains no suggestion of the struggle for faith apparent in the early poems. It is decorous, easy, and produces ornamental rather than revelatory effects. "Poem in October" is a work of consummate finish. But it is a leap of the heart, not of the spirit. In articulating joy, it does not pretend to engage in the search for a spiritual rationale which occupies Thomas in his earlier poems.

"Fern Hill" is cut of the same cloth as "Poem in October." Its setting is pastoral; its style is elaborate, but not provocatively unconventional; it depends for much of its effect on subtle, flowing rhythms and near-rhymes. It is a poem of animals, particularly farm animals, while "Poem in October" is filled with birds. In its praise of the experiences of childhood and in the note struck in ". . . the sabbath rang slowly/In the pebbles of the holy streams," it corresponds closely with the devotional mood of "Poem in October." Unlike "Poem in October," however, it does not report a particular experience or insight; it is simply an older man's recollection and evaluation of the joys of a country childhood. The view expressed amounts to Blake's aphorism, "Time is the mercy of eternity," for in its last lines, "Time held me green and dying,/Though I sang in my chains like the sea," all the pleasures described are suddenly put into their place as a stage in the predetermined cycle which the mercy of time has permitted. The acceptance of death would be more convincing as a spiritual triumph if it were preceded by evidence of resistance; but the transition from joy in life to resignation to death is smooth and untroubled, so that the two form a single mood.

[120]

"Fern Hill" is probably the best example of the easy, supple, wandering style Thomas developed by the hard work of his later years. It is still under absolute control, as the complicated matching stanzas and fastidious word choices clearly show; but it is a control that favors longer and less densely organized units and that seeks clarity rather than multiplicity of meaning. It moves in a horizontal rather than a vertical dimension. The expansiveness appears, not only in the meter and syntax, but also in the imagery, which deals in correspondences that are neither strongly insisted on nor strongly evocative. Such locutions as "the heydays of his eyes" and "windfall light" are little more than exuberant, almost jocular, word plays without sustained emphasis. When the poet says of the morning freshness of the farm, "it was Adam and maiden," Thomas is exploiting only the surface of this loosely organized phrase, not its mythic depths.

As a catalog of a child's country joys, "Fern Hill" is unexceptional; an unfortunate element is the personification of time which is central to its structure and is extended throughout the poem. The world of the early poems is approached twice in "Fern Hill"; first, when speaking of morning on the farm, Thomas says, "So it must have been after the birth of the simple light/In the first, spinning place. . . ." In these lines the union of past and present is full of a naïve radiance; And secondly, in the final lines, where the awkwardly personified time, the commonplace notion of "chains," and the surrealistic image of the boy as a singing, but enchained sea appear. This sudden complexity is out of keeping with the rest of the poem, and, on the whole, excessively intricate for the meanings it conveys.

According to Bill Read, "Poem on His Birthday" was intended to express the ambivalence felt toward the joys of the visible world by a poet who has reached the Biblical midpoint, the age of thirty-five.[2] Though written after "Over Sir John's hill," it logically comes next in the sequence; for the acknowledgment that death is part of nature's cycle, which is nearly suppressed in "Poem in October" and in "Fern Hill," now emerges to occupy a conspicuous place in a poem which still amounts essentially to a hymn of praise. The poem reflects the duel between resistance and acceptance that might be expected as the result of a reversion to the dialectic vision of the earlier poems. Up to the ninth stanza, where a turning point is found, the poet's surroundings reflect the threat of approaching death. Like the instinct-driven creatures of the littoral, he must move toward the final entrapment, "the ambush of his wounds." And though to die is to approach God, still, "dark is a long way." A spontaneous, paradoxical, and irrational recovery takes place with "Yet, though I cry with tumbledown tongue,/ Count my blessings aloud. . . ." as the poet reflects that he shares the life of the sea, and that his enjoyment of sensuous experience increases as he grows older, becoming in itself a spiritual resource. Hence, at the end of the poem, he feels that he can meet death without resistance.

The joy of existence praised spontaneously and for its own sake in "Poem in October" and in "Fern Hill" appears in "Poem on His Birthday" as one-half of the balance found in experience: a compensation for mortality, a rationalization of death. Though the poem is set in nature, it dwells on the insufficiency of nature; most of its praise is for the unseen godhead behind nature. For the natural world found in this poem is not the intimate, companionable realm of the two earlier odes but one of predators, catastrophes, and destruction. Blood-glutted seals and bone-littered beaches are among the images that recall the struggle for existence. This birthday is not, as those in earlier poems were, an occasion for rejoicing but a step toward the death the poet sees in the nature about him, in "the claw tracks of hawks," in the sunken ships, and in the hunting seals. Even the herons, who retain the sacerdotal guise they have had in the two earlier odes, now seem to wear the minnows that surround them as a shroud. The notion that the swinging waves ring a silent angelus brings to mind the "sunken cathedral" motif with its complex spiritual implications. A general decline of nature is suggested by the ship-wrecking sea and by the falling stars; the scene evokes a despair relieved only by union with "fabulous, dear God" who can somehow turn death into a matter for joy. The inadequacy of mortal life is brilliantly expressed in the description of the shore in stanza seven as a kind of Golgotha littered with the detritus of sea life—"Marrow of eagles, the roots of whales/And wishbones of wild geese"—but also reflecting the presence of God. The eighth stanza acknowledges the elemental contest of earth, wind, and sea in a passage that corresponds exactly to the thought of Robert Frost's wry

> ... it looked as if
> The shore was lucky in being backed by cliff,
> The cliff in being backed by continent. ...

But this vision of Thomas' is also accompanied by prayer. These balances of the destruction apparent in the life of the shore with the deliverance felt beyond it culminate, at the reversal of stanza nine, in a long period of paradoxical praise and thanks. Through a sequence of ideas resembling sequences of Hopkins (though it does not arrive at his ultimate rejection of sensuous pleasure), the sensuous in nature, rendered increasingly precious by the approach of death, is intensified into holiness. And this growing significance of the visible world is taken, paradoxically, as meaning that it will not be lost in death, but that "The mansouled fiery islands" of the poem's setting will be revealed in a more glorious form, "spanned with angels." In the homely "Count my blessings aloud," interpreted literally in "Four elements and five/Senses . . . ," Thomas is attempting one of those witty resuscitations of cliché occasionally found in his earlier poems. Also reminiscent of his earlier style is the ingenious insertion of a familiar sacramental phrase into ". . . and man a spirit in love . . ./To his nimbus bell cool kingdom come. . . ." as the poem slopes upward to its closing assertion of faith.

II

Thomas described "Over Sir John's hill," together with "In Country Sleep" and "In the White Giant's Thigh," as part of a "grand and simple" projected poem to be called "In Country Heaven."[3] This large work was to be about the renewal of the earth after some mysterious universal catastrophe. If the four odelike poems are to be regarded as a sequence, "Over Sir John's hill" comes after "Poem on His Birthday," though it was written earlier. The freely flowing joy and naïve piety of the other odes are now balanced against contrary feelings. In this poem, Thomas reads a pattern of divine justice from the landscape and animal life of Laugharne. Both the blood lust of the hawk and the suffering of the birds who are his prey are accepted as parts of the design of nature, equally wonderful and admirable. The austerities of *18 Poems* and the compassion of the wartime poems are both present and are resolved, through the rhetorical structure of the poem, into a coherent moral view. Further, the point of view in the poem is detached and objective; Thomas does not reduce the spectacle of nature to a reflection of personal conflicts but puts himself into the poem as a recorder, "young Aesop fabling," who sympathetically writes down the chronicle of the ordeal imposed by nature upon its creatures.

Like the other odes, "Over Sir John's hill" is a *tour de force* of metrical ingenuity. The twelve lines of its stanzas range in length from one syllable to fourteen, and there is an intricate rhyme scheme that employs assonance as well as rhyme. The stanzas are nearly uniform with each other, syllable by syllable, and the corresponding lines often have identical metrical patterns; three of the stanzas end in present participles.[4] The rhythm of each stanza is made to approach and recede from the one-syllable line in the middle. Over this complicated and beautiful metric structure long sentences wash in a rhythm of their own like breakers over a pattern of stones, yielding excellent effects of harmony, contrast, climax, approach, and return. The description of the birds in the first three stanzas, for example, has an independent structure that sets up a counterpoint with the stanzaic structure. The syntactical units are free of the metrical ones, except that they terminate at the ends of lines. A series of vivid words establishes its own sequence at the beginning of certain lines until the climactic "Death" appears, not at the conclusion, but at the beginning of a stanza, where the verse remains poised for a further ascent.

The rhetoric of the poem corresponds with this resourceful and controlled metric structure.[5] Through an apparatus of intellectually conceived and deliberately sustained metaphysical imagery, Thomas makes the point that the spectacle of nature is just and orderly. The landscape about Laugharne is seen as a court of law. When the jackdaws hover over the top of "judging Sir John's elmed Hill," the hill becomes a magistrate who puts on his black cap to pronounce a capital sentence. His executioner is the hawk and his prisoners are the "led-astray birds," who ". . . squawk/To fiery tyburn" as the hawk, hovering "at halter height," seems to draw them upward "to his claws/

And gallows." The mercy of God is invoked for the victims, but the hawk is also admired for his energy that burns, like a fire, to set off the fuse of the birds' doom. The fire image, sustained through the first part of the poem, recalls the explosion imagery of *18 Poems*, with its ambivalent suggestions of creative and destructive power. Mourning witnesses are present at this judgment, the poet and the sober, holy herons that pervade the four odes; but "the tear of the Towy" and the hooting of the owl also express nature's sorrow at the fate of the little birds. A remarkable drama of sounds accompanies this enactment of justice; after the squawking of the victims comes the sudden concussion of execution in the crash, flash, whack of various movements of birds. The call of the hawk is echoed by the call of the chicks accepting their fate, and the whistling of the birds is recalled as a prayer is said for them. The sounds after the death are the hooting of the owl, "a grassblade blown in cupped hands," the dabbling of herons in the water, and the slow sounds of the river which the poet records as a memorial for the dead birds.

III

As we have seen, Thomas seems to have intended to link "In Country Sleep" and "In the White Giant's Thigh" with "Over Sir John's hill" as parts of a single long poem. In any event, they belong with the sequence of four odes by virtue of their bucolic atmosphere and poetic style. The two poems are on contrasting themes, but they are similar in setting and structure. Each is essentially a catalog of images and impressions loosely held within a sprawling syntactic framework. The obtrusive musical effects Thomas favored at this period are present, and the poems also exhibit numerous ingenuities, witty intersections of meaning, and pithy turns of phrase. These elements, organized in complex profusion, obscure a thin thread of statement which wanders through each of the poems and which turns out, upon examination, to be somewhat slight for the heavy weight of example and allusion it bears.

Like "Poem in October" and "Fern Hill," "In Country Sleep" is occupied with the Wordsworthian theme of the loss of the imaginative powers of childhood. The father, meditating over his sleeping daughter, prays that she will retain her capacity for vision and innocence in spite of the hazards they entail. The vague "faith" he hopes she will preserve and the holiness associated with the sheltering countryside are not linked to any specific beliefs but to the capacity for belief itself. This seems clear from the fact that the countryside which is invoked as the visible counterpart of the realm of imagination, ". . . that country kind" and "the green good," is associated with three separate provinces of imaginative thought. It is sacramental, for it has "the rain telling its beads" and "the prayer wheeling moon"; but it is also the world of fairy stories, the "shire/Of the hobnail tales"; and it is also seen as a part of Thomas' peculiar visionary universe, for he exclaims on the "Pastoral beat of blood through the laced leaves!"

It is not surprising that there should be some difference of opinion among the critics as to the identity of the threatening "Thief," for he is associated with Christ and holiness on the one hand, and with the sinfulness of the intellect on the other.[6] The series of exclamations that introduces Part II warns that the Thief is inherent in the vitality, energy, and, most interestingly, in the sacredness of nature, for he is heard in

the rooks

> Cawing from their black bethels soaring, the holy books
> Of birds!

The abundance of imagery related to him demonstrates, first, that he is holy:

The sermon

> Of blood! The bird loud vein! The saga from mermen
> To seraphim
> Leaping! The gospel rooks! All tell, this night, of him. . . .

But other parts of this imagery also insist on two other attributes: "falling" and orderliness. The Thief is associated, for example, particularly in Part II, with things that are regulated and that fall: "the designed snow," "the dew's ruly sea," and "the ship shape cloud." Associations with the Fall seem irre-

sistible here, but it is also clear that the Thief is responsible
for the dwindling of imagination mentioned in "I, in my intricate
image" as "the fortune of manhood; the natural peril." The
poet's daughter, who is threatened by the Thief is, like him,
a part of nature:

> Music of elements, that a miracle makes!
> Earth, air, water, fire, singing into the white act,
>
> The haygold haired, my love asleep. . . .

In spite of the danger he represents, and the father's knowledge
that he will abandon her, the girl longs for the Thief, and the
father assures her that "My dear this night he comes and night
without end my dear." But her "faith" will survive the encroach-
ments of maturity represented by the Thief, just as the "ruled
sun," in spite of its regularity, continues to pour forth its energy.

"In the White Giant's Thigh" is a meditation upon the procreative, rather than the imaginative manifestation of the universe's vitality. It is supposed to be occasioned by the graves
of countrywomen buried near a male figure worked into a
chalk hillside by prehistoric people as a fertility symbol. (A
well-known example of this type of primitive art is the Cerne
Giant, near Cerne Abbas in Dorset.) The poet imagines that
the women were promiscuous but childless, and he memorial-
izes their vitality by means of the paradox that their fertility
survives through the memory of their many loves. A review of
the seasonal loves of the women leads Thomas through a number of vivid and translucent miniatures of country wooing, resembling the indiscriminate affections of Poll Garter in *Under
Milk Wood*. The way is prepared for the notion that the vitality
of the women endures by an allusion to the timelessness of the
natural cycle in "The dust of their kettles and clocks swings
to and fro/Where the hay rides now. . . ."

The poem begins by dwelling on the pathos of the fact that
the women were denied the children they wanted, but this is
soon outbalanced by the primeval vigor and sustained rhythms
with which their rustic dalliance is described. As always in
Thomas, the nearness of the country means the nearness of
procreative vitality, so that the scenes of human flirtation are

set against a background of "vaulting does" and "horned bucks."
Human love is merged with animal copulation in an image
where the clodhopper Ledas take a humble variant of the swan,
"under their gander king/Trounced by his wings in the hissing
shippen. . . ." Since their loves are a part of the greater vitality
of nature, concludes the poem, "the daughters of darkness flame
like Fawkes fires still."

CHAPTER 7

Longer Poems

I

IT is surprising, considering the consistency of his poetic habits and the narrowness of his range, that Thomas' four longer poems should exhibit such wide differences in subject and style. The "Altarwise by owl-light" sequence is an intricately ambiguous, punning fabric in which Thomas carries his linguistic and rhetorical virtuosity to extremes, producing a result both more complex and more obscure than any of the other works. "The Ballad of the Long-Legged Bait" is a lighthearted, nimble, and fantastic narrative depending primarily on symbolic and allegorical events, though it does have some of Thomas' private verbal and metaphoric effects. "A Winter's Tale" bears some resemblance to his prose fantasies. It combines realistic and imaginary elements in a verse narrative, free of linguistic ingenuities, which embodies some of the constants of myth and folklore. Finally, "Vision and Prayer" resembles some of the other poems dealing with childbirth as a promise of spiritual deliverance, but it is a fuller development of this theme, involving a process of conversion; and it has, in addition, the device, used nowhere else by Thomas, of shaped stanzas.

It might be said that the four longer poems, in spite of stylistic differences, are in a general way devoted to the same theme: death and resurrection. The pattern is perfectly explicit in three, "Altarwise . . . ," "The Ballad of the Long-Legged Bait," and "A Winter's Tale." In each of these a personage is sacrificed for the sake of a larger life to follow from his death. The subject of "Altarwise . . ." is the death of Jesus; in "The Ballad" the bait is cast to the fish, but returns home in a changed form with the fisherman; and in "A Winter's Tale" the man who pursues the bird dies for the sake of mystic union with her. In "Vision and Prayer" the life and death are only spiritual; the speaker rejects salvation, but then changes his mind. On this metaphoric level, then, the pattern is the same, and it is one consistent with the dialectic reality of Thomas' early poems.

The series of ten sonnetlike poems called "Altarwise by owl-light," the most ambitious composition of Thomas' early career, is also the most controversial and obscure. All that is reasonably clear is that it concerns the crucifixion and the resurrection as foci of spiritual conflict. It would be difficult to say whether the Biblical episodes are the subject or are used symbolically, or even whether the separate poems are consistent in this regard. Olson and Tindall have worked out detailed readings of the sequence as a whole, and H. H. Kleinman has devoted *The Religious Sonnets of Dylan Thomas* to a thorough explication, together with very full information about possible sources and analogues. The poem is so elusive that these three studies agree only in minor points, and they are very far apart in their views of its structure, import, and symbolism.[1] The critics are divided even about the genre to which the sequence should be assigned. Olson thinks it is a "meditation"; Tindall considers it a narrative; Marshall W. Stearns does not believe the poems are closely unified at all; and Kleinman thinks each is a "tableau" of one part of Christ's story. Certainly the sections differ in mode; some are descriptive, some discursive, and some apparently narrative. Perhaps these and many other questions would be answerable if "Altarwise . . ." were a finished poem; for its ten parts, according to Thomas, are only the first sections of what was to have been a longer work.

Olson interprets the sequence as a confrontation of the reality of sin, ending with the perception that sin is ". . . to a merciful God nothing but the necessary condition of mercy."[2] According to him, the symbols implementing this train of thought are referable to six different levels of interpretation, including the seasons of the year, Greek mythology, and Christian legend. The most remarkable of these sources of imagery is astrology; the progress of the poem corresponds with a "long march of constellations" which supplies much of the background of reference and allusion. The speaker of the poem uses the movements of the heavenly bodies, particularly the constellation of Hercules and the sun (which are identifiable with each other) and the constellation Cygnus, the cross, to express his thoughts about sin and redemption. The "half-way" house of the first poem is the autumnal equinox, and the "gentleman" who is "altarwise" is the sun which, as the year progresses, moves southward toward Ara, the Altar. The sequence is organized around two journeys across the sky: that of the constellation Hercules, associated with the pagan world and its sinfulness, which ends in Section V; and that of Cygnus, the Northern Cross, which begins in Section VII. Thus, the movement of the skies corresponds, first to the speaker's fear of death and then to his salvation.

It would be easier to dismiss the exquisite ingenuities on which Olson's analysis depends if Thomas' associative methods were not equally arbitrary. However, Olson's imaginativeness does not quite correspond with that of Thomas. Thomas was capable of making allusions to bodies of legend and to recondite lore, and even of working out sustained images involving them; but he would not be expected to weave his verse over the lattice of a prepared framework of information as Olson supposes him to be doing here. Olson's zodiacal parallels account for much, but they do not always render the text intelligible. Further, his admission that Section IV stands apart from the astrological fable altogether, and his failure to explain many obscurities are, considering the extreme exegetical measures to which he resorts, not reassuring.

Tindall reads the poem as an autobiography narrated through a particularly rich apparatus of metaphor and allusion. "Beginning with his begetting," he says, "the story proceeds through childhood, and ends with the writing and publication of his poems."[3] The Holy Family is a counterpart of the group formed by Thomas and his parents, and the Biblical imagery and allusions are metaphors for the Oedipal and spiritual suffering going on within it. The figures of Mary, the furies, and the "black medusa" refer to the maternal aspect of this pattern; the "gentleman," the devil, the old cock, and Adam refer to the paternal one. Much of the imagery, in Tindall's analysis, is concerned with generation and parenthood; the grave, the "Christward shelter," the "bread-sided field," and the "undertaker's van," for example, he takes to be allusions to the womb; the cross, the "long stick" of Section II and the poker of Section IV are phallic.

Kleinman thinks of the sequence as a series of more or less

distinct scenes "moving from the Incarnation through the Crucifixion to an apocalyptic prophecy"[4] and reflecting the spirit
of seventeenth-century devotional literature in mood and
imagery. Its obscurities, as he explains them, are, in the main,
due to the fact that it is a tissue of echoes and allusions to a
wide range of learned and literary works. A good part of his
study is therefore occupied with possible sources and analogues
for Thomas' language and imagery. Among these are the *Zohar;*
Moby Dick; the sermons of Hugh Latimer and Lancelot And-
rewes; the works of the Egyptologist, E. A. W. Budge; and certain
practical arts, such as gardening, fishing, and bookbinding. This
exhaustive explication is somewhat indiscriminate, and, as Kleinman leaves it, it does not help the reader to assess the poem as
a whole; but it does clarify many enigmatic images and allusions.

Even the most determined analysts of the "Altarwise . . ."
sequence admit that their conclusions are only provisional.
The difficulty is that the language and the imagery of the
poem do not seem to refer to explicable ideas. Thomas once
sharply corrected some remarks made by Edith Sitwell about
one of the images in the first section of "Altarwise . . . ," and he
issued his famous prohibition against bypassing the literal meanings of his poetry in favor of more general and familiar ones;
yet his own explanation is hardly less obscure than the original
passage. Any prose meaning that might be abstracted from a
given passage is little more than a guide or channel for the
images that carry the real thoughts; and the multiplicity and
complexity of the particulars attached to these thoughts resist
explication even more stubbornly than the other early poems.

The difficulty can be illustrated by the two lines that end
the third section: "We rung our weathering changes on the
ladder,/Said the antipodes, and twice spring chimed." Reduced
sharply to their simplest sense, the two lines probably mean no
more than "There was a second spring in the southern hemis-
phere," an event related through metaphor and the emphasis on
seasonal change found in primitive religion, to the second spring
of the resurrection.

This sufficiently oblique connection is complicated by a number of elements brought into the lines through ingenious and
unconventional uses of language and imagery. The story of

"weathering changes" begins with the phrase "wood of weathers" in the last line of the preceding section, in which "weathers" carries two of Thomas' associations, winds and seasons, both related to religious ideas. Winds are forceful but invisible, like the power of the spirit; the seasons represent spiritual changes, winter being associated with sin and death, and spring with love and fertility. In the following section, this imagery leads to a discussion of the relation between the seasons of the year and spiritual vitality, and introduces not only the "three dead seasons," but also "Adam's wether" and the series of words relating to sheep, including "lamb . . . butt . . . horned. . . ram . . . mutton fold" in which the various kinds of animals seem to be associated both with the seasons, or "weathers," and with spiritual states. The black ram is winter, and it is when he is alive that the second spring of the south "chimes." In the passage under discussion, then, "weathering"—having passed from its meaning of "seasons" through an association with sheep representing seasons—returns to a meaning approximating its original significance with the added support of the image of the church bell implied in "rung," "changes," and "chimed." Thus, "weathering changes" musters a scattered range of imagery to mean changes of both seasons and the spirit.

The ladder presents a complex of associations no less formidable. It refers back to the passage in Section II where the image of a ladder made of "cross-bones of Abaddon" and "verticals of Adam," resembling both the ladder of Jacob and the cross, serves as a means of ascent to the stars, an episode that certainly seems to allude to the death of Christ and his ascent to heaven.[5] Hence, the ladder in our passage is, in one sense, the upper air since it leads upward; and, in another, it is a physical symbol of spiritual aspiration, the cross or Jacob's ladder. In "rung," Thomas has done violence to grammar for the sake of a pun drawing "weathering changes" and "ladder" together. The statement of the antipodes therefore means both "We produced various seasons of the year in the atmosphere" and "We went through the various spiritual states leading to salvation," the first acting as a metaphoric vehicle for the second.

Not only do the words in these lines have numerous meanings, but their significances arise from their context, not from common use. Such words as "rung," "weathering," "ladder," and "chimed" have so little to do with the meanings assigned to them by conventional usage that it is not too much to say that, in employing them as he does, Thomas is speaking a language of his own. Further, the metaphors overlap and obscure each other, as Christine Brooke-Rose has observed; and the passage suggests many ideas without presenting any one of them fully. Whatever its capacity for capturing the complexity of spiritual experience may be, this style clearly tends to sacrifice in clarity what it gains in import, so that it sometimes becomes impossible to identify a prose meaning that will serve to control and unify its effects.

II

As Ralph Maud has observed, the subject of the "Altarwise . . ." sequence as a whole may be stated as the first line of the eighth section, "This was the crucifixion on the mountain."[6] The opening of the sequence is certainly occupied with the crucifixion, either as an event or as a metaphor. The "gentleman" is readily identifiable with Christ; in the compressed cosmic dialect of the sequence, which freely admits inconsistencies of tone and solecisms, he lies "graveward"—that is, he is dying; and "altarwise," that is, he is an object of worship. The fact that he is being deprived of his vitality is conveyed through the castrating image of the mandrake; but this action also means, according to Thomas himself, that "the horror of tomorrow" is being bitten out of the "gentleman's" loins.[7] Thus, the poem opens with a grotesque act of destruction that also means salvation.

"Abaddon in the hangnail cracked from Adam" is a typical imperfectly integrated duality. Abaddon is the destructive angel of the Hebrew underworld, and one of the things the line is saying is that Adam's sin gave birth to him. But the word "hangnail" is interesting as an example of a rhetorical peculiarity of this sequence: a pun is used to bring together and to identify with each other two separate objects or events. Thomas' idea that the fingernail is associated with death or decline is a persistent relationship, rationalized in a variety of ways. There are "the worm beneath the nail" in "If I were tickled by the rub of love," the notion of the fingernail as a half-moon in the story, "The Orchards," and the line "Glory cracked like a flea" from "A saint about to fall." It was from Adam's fingernail, then, that the spirit of evil emerged. But it is also present in the "hangnail" that fixes Jesus to the cross. In this way, the word establishes a significant parallel between the two supreme sins: the Fall and the execution of Christ.

The last eight lines pursue the idea that the dead Christ spoke to the infant poet, and declared that he was a permanent part of the heavens, like the constellations. The imagery, though grotesque, is far from haphazard. It is formed of irrational associations shrewdly woven into a continuous fabric of reciprocal meanings. The allusions to chickens, and the description of the cross standing "on one leg," the conjunction of "cradle" with "bed" and "heaven's egg" with the constellations suggest but do not exhaust the intricate relationships that are present.

Section II consists of a series of assertions about the essential unity of the universe. These observations—that the child soon grows up, that the spark of conception lights a fire which traverses the "long stick" of the ladder from earth to heaven, and, finally, that the body is identical with the earth and its plants and birds—are commentaries about the significance of the crucifixion in the previous section. Kleinman points out (24-25) that the pelican is a traditional symbol for Christ. There is some question about the "you" to whom the poem is addressed; Kleinman thinks it introduces an ironic apostrophe to God; Olson, who thinks it means the sun, believes that the lines in question describe the movements of the sun through the heavens:

> The horizontal cross-bones of Abaddon,
> You by the cavern over the black stairs,
> Rung bone and blade, the verticals of Adam,
> And, manned by midnight, Jacob to the stars.

These lines are worth careful analysis, for they illustrate the problems typical of the poem as a whole. A possible reading would take "you" as Jesus, and the action described as a metaphor for the ascent of his soul from the cross. He has climbed to heaven on a ladder whose rungs are formed of the bones of Abaddon and whose sides are "of Adam." A radical transference occurs with "Jacob," which is not only a verb meaning "climb," but, it is clear, a verb in the past tense. But this single meaning, which might be approached through a rearrangement of the order of the sentence ("You . . . rung . . . the horizontal . . . the verticals . . . and . . . Jacob to the stars"), is accompanied by a number of subsidiary ones. The ladder is not only the ladder of Jacob but also the cross; for the horizontals are "cross-bones." "Rung" is not only a noun, with relation to the unstated idea of ladder, but also a verb with relation to "blade," and possibly an adjective with relation to "bone"; yet none of these senses really satisfies the requirements of the sentence as a whole, which calls for a verb meaning "climbed," or, at least, "touched."[8]

Hence, this passage has a number of meanings: Jesus, Jacob, Adam, Abaddon; the ladder, the ringing blade, the cross, the cavern, the stairs; Jacob's dream, the crucifixion, the Fall—all of these are present, interlocking, partially obscuring each other, so that it is impossible to say that the passage is finally about any one of them, or to distinguish what is metaphoric from what is literal. Thomas is not saying one thing completely, but rather saying several things at once, all more or less incompletely, so that individual words and images, while carrying numerous meanings, do not always satisfy the requirements of any one statement that might be abstracted from them. The final four lines of the section revert to an aspect of the body-earth metaphor; Jesus is hearing that he and the earth share the same capacities for life and, as suggested by the hemlock, for death.

One of the serious problems of the sequence is the identity of the speakers and the persons being addressed. These roles seem to be filled at various times by God, Mary, Jesus, Hercules, and the poet himself; and there can be no objection, in view of Thomas' style, to considering them composites of all of these. In Section I, the poet seems to be speaking and quoting Christ in the last two lines; but the latter part of Section III seems to be spoken by Christ himself, appearing, in a marvelous verbal play, as a dissipating corpse, a "rip of the vaults," and as Rip van Winkle, who also awoke after a long sleep. In the first six lines, the combat of good and evil is played out among images of sheep; Christ, the lamb, has been "horned down" by the sinful Adam. The "marrow-ladle" is a fascinating enigma, for which Thomas' other uses of "marrow" fail to supply a solution. Olson fits it nicely into his astrological reading by identifying it with Sagittarius, the "Milk-Dipper." Tindall, stressing the surrealist quality of the image, takes the van to be the womb and the ladle to be the phallus. Whatever its obscurity, the passage has echoes relating it to other parts of the poem; "marrow" is connected with "bone," "ladle" with "dipped," "wrinkled" and "van" with "Rip Van Winkle." The action, "Dipped me breast-deep in the descended bone" is parallel to the resurrection reflected in the last two lines; the Christ figure has unified life and death, just as winter and spring can both be present on the earth.

Section IV, with its long series of enigmatic questions, has been given sharply differing interpretations. To Tindall the section represents the point in the development of the child when he asks embarrassing questions about sex and birth; he takes the lines beginning "Button your bodice" for a warning that prudery will not conceal the truth. Olson, who regards this section as a departure from the astrological scheme he sees in the sequence as a whole, interprets the questions as probings of faith. "Questions are hunchbacks to the poker marrow" is then a disparaging comment about crooked skeptics as compared with straightforward believers; and "Button your bodice" is the beginning of an ironic assurance that these doubts cannot be justified but that the "camel's eye" of faith will save the skeptic in spite of himself. Kleinman, somewhat similarly, thinks the questions are impatient queries asked of the infant Jesus, and that each has its own theological bearing. The parenthetical lines are Jesus' remarks and the line about hunchbacks and the poker, as in Olson's reading, compares the doubt expressed in the questions to the directness of belief. He interprets the last four lines as an account of the Nativity being photographed; but all that seems really clear is that Thomas is playing his verbal games vigorously; not only does most of the vocabulary, including "close-up" and "cutting" reflect notions of photography and motion pictures, but the adjective *"arc*-lamped" relates this area of imagery to the "flood."[9]

Section V is about deception, defeat, and subjection; but the Wild West imagery with which it opens establishes a riotously humorous tone. These lines, says Tindall, mean that the child has now reached the stage of playing as "Marshal Dylan of Dodge City." The religious and Biblical substance of this section is clothed in the vivid costumes of the motion pictures alluded to in the closing lines of Section IV. Playing cards for salvation in a frontier saloon, the poet has been tricked by those two sharpers, Gabriel and Jesu. In his despair, he enters a stage that might be compared with the mystic phase of the "dark night of the soul." The consequent exile, wandering, and desolation are conveyed through a complex of allusions to a series of outcasts, the two Ishmaels (the Biblical one and Melville's), Jonah and Ulysses, and to the "waste seas" of the frozen north. "Pin-legged" means that the angel's legs were pinned or nailed to the cross and that the angel with whom Adam was confronted was Jesus. If the passage from Virgil cited by the white bear is from the fourth Eclogue, which has been interpreted as foretelling the coming of Christ, the section may well end on a note of hope.

Sections VI and VII are both about language: the first is about its perverting capacities; the second, about its holiness as one of the original constituents of the natural order. The sacrifices of eye and tongue offered in Section VI are made in the interests of purifying the means of perception and expression, for the "sea eye" and the "fork tongue" are to be severed. The sea, "an evil index," is associated here with sin and destruction; and the running imagery persistently exhibits the idea that language has been drenched with the corrupting sea water. The crater that gives light is "tide-traced," the words have "oyster vowels," and burn "sea silence"; and Adam, who was "salt Adam" in Section V, "Spelt out the seven seas," which are "an evil *index*." This association of words and the sea projects a notion of a kind of language, which is, like the work of the scholars and archaeologists in Section IX, futile and misleading. Another thread of sustained imagery is the familiar identification of wax with flesh; the consequences of this are "tallow-eyed"; the candle, of which the wick must be a part; and "the wound of man-wax." "Tallow I" is not only a crafty echo of "tallow-eyed" but also, it should be noted, an adjective modifying a pronoun. "The fats of midnight" and the "wax's tower" seem to refer, as they do in "A grief ago," to the act of making love.

The action of Section VI, therefore, seems to begin with the poet writing; then the sacrifice is offered and executed by love and the "old cock," after which an act of physical love takes place. But there is no change yet. Adam, the figure of the Fall, still speaks corrupting doctrine; and the celebrated grotesque "bagpipe-breasted ladies" continue "Time's tune" of "heart-break" as it is called in Section VII. This final image creates a remarkable effect, at once momentous and enigmatic, vivid and obscure. Standing alone, it is enough to convey the sense of some horrible event; but every element in the image can be justified—according to Thomas' methods of association—in terms of other contexts in the sequence. In fact, these relationships account for much of the obscurity found here. The ladies are the sirens of the preceding and following sections, the "deadweed" is the vegetation of the sinister sea, the "manwax" is the candle of fertility that appears a few lines earlier, and the wound is that of Jesus. In the action of these last two lines, the ladies are at once extinguishing the candle and extracting from Jesus' suf-fering the "blood gauze," the sterile doctrine of continued life elaborated in Section IX as "Death from a bandage" and as "the linen spirit."

Section VII views nature as a realm of meaningful symbols; both the "book of water" in Section VI and "the book of trees" in Section VII continue the language imagery of "Especially when the October wind." Conrad Aiken praised the first six lines of this section, which ends with the curse, "Doom on deniers at the wind-turned statement," as a defense of eloquence: "It is the answer . . . to all the jejune precisionism, and dreary ironic defeatism, of the past generation. . . ."[10] But this section is also an injunction to heed the language of nature and to beware of the "music" of the furies who measure Time, rendering it as bitter as the sponge offered to Jesus, a force exercising des-tructive power over things that are both beautiful and brief, "man and cloud," and "rose and icicle."

Section VIII clearly presents a specific scene; although it has been a favorite subject of analysis, it contains a number of elements that have never been satisfactorily explained. Typical of the prevailing dissension is the question of the identity of the speaker: to Stearns, the poem is spoken by Mary; to Francis Scarfe, the speaker is Christ; to Tindall he is the poet, who identifies himself at different times with both. The momentous but obscure event of the last four lines is, according to Scarfe, "the birth of love through the death of sex." Stearns offers two interpretations of the transformation witnessed here by Mary: either she gives up her claim to motherhood as she sees her son's body "unsexed," that is, passing from mortal life into immortality; or she exchanges her role as the mother of a man for a new one as the mother of God.[11]

The critics do agree in identifying "Time's nerve in vinegar" as Jesus, and this epithet links the poem with destructive Time and with the image of the sponge in Section VII. Images from the crucifixion pervade this section; Jesus' suffering on behalf of the world is his "wound," the tears are not only thorns but the "pins" that fasten him to the cross, and Mary is stooped over like the three bent crosses that stood at Golgotha. The rainbow that springs from her nipples (perhaps the Christianized sign of God's covenant with Noah) is Christ, who brings deliverance to a slowly awakening world. The speaker of the last four lines is an agent of sacrifice, a surgeon who performs the self-tormenting operation of atonement and suffers "the heaven's children." Whether Mary can be said to fill this role is dubious. The remarkable clause, "unsex the skeleton," describing the crisis at Christ's death has been variously interpreted; but it has a possible source, mentioned by Kleinman, in James Thomson's "City of Dreadful Night," in which the phantoms roaming the streets immodestly reveal themselves uncovered by the funerary decencies:

> The nudity of flesh will blush, though tameless,
> The extreme nudity of bone grins shameless,
> The unsexed skeleton mocks shroud and pall.[12]

Thomson's skeleton is not castrated but stripped of flesh to emphasize the horror of death by its "extreme nudity of bone," an action perfectly appropriate to the "sawbones" of Thomas' passage.

The two concluding sections contrast false and true traditions derived from the scene of the crucifixion described in Section VIII. Olson is undoubtedly correct in interpreting the seventh line of Section IX—"This was the resurrection in the desert"—as ironic. Imagery of scholarship and mummification (both associated with Egypt and its ineffectual notion of immortality) and the "linen spirit" of the preservation of what is dead describe a false renewal. Such paraphernalia merely "weds my long gentleman to dusts and furies" and belies the true spirit of Christ, rendering it sterile and vengeful. It seems clear that Thomas is referring to the perversions of religion by formalism and dogma. Since Christ's sacrifice, distorted by this tradition, has become futile, the symbol of it (his "wound") is now to be interred with suitable trappings in the "triangle landscape" of the pyramids, the great cemetery of Egypt.

The vivid image that concludes Section X and the sequence as a whole exploits the duality of the crucifixion; the death of Christ is the deliverance of mankind.

> . . . that Day
> When the worm builds with the gold straws of venom
> My nest of mercies in the rude, red tree.

These lines are a particularly good example of Thomas' deft way of accommodating his metaphors to one another. The image of the nest is no doubt suggested by the "tree," and the straws are entirely logical. But in the early poem, "When once the twilight locks," the straws are associated with lack of faith, "the straws of sleep"; and in the sequence itself they appear as the "sea-straw" and "deadweed" associated with the sterility of the sea. Hence the renewal of spiritual life through death is perfectly reflected by the worms and the straw combining to fashion the "nest of mercies." Unfortunately, the earlier lines of this section are less clear. The "tale's sailor" must be Odysseus, recalling the "stones of odyssey" in Section IX, but he is now on a Christian voyage, and refrains from entering a "dummy bay." A possible reading here is a refusal to accept death as final; the death conceived on earth is a "dummy bay," a false haven, and no real ending to the voyage. Instead, salvation is to be found on the sea in the course of the journey. A mysterious speaker asks a mysterious question about a "rhubarb man." The person he asks it of, the "tall fish," can readily be identified as Christ; the initials of a Greek title applied to Christ approximate the word *ichthys*, or fish, and led to the use of the fish as a familiar symbol for Christ. The garden of the fall weirdly hovers around the "sea-ghost," the soul of the dead Jesus. And the sequence ends as the poet asks that the renewal of the primitive joy of Eden may move toward the Day of Judgment.

There are, of course, numerous relationships that knit the sequence as a whole into a single fabric and fix the order of its sections, but I do not think any logical development is to be found in it. In the first section, the infant hears Christ "scraping" at his cradle; in the final one, the poet hopes for deliverance through the drama of the cross. There has been no clear progression or reversal here, such as would characterize a narrative. Further, the dimension of time necessary for narrative seems to be lacking; this is rather the static, swirling, nebula-like reality recognizable as the environment of *18 Poems*. The rhetoric tells us that hope is implicit in suffering and that renewal is implicit in death; but while the crucifixion is described, the resurrection is not. Hence, the expectation of the "nest of mercies" is a matter of faith; the action of the poem is psychological and confirmation by actual developments is deferred. In spite of its local obscurities, the sequence does have a definable theme, a surprisingly familiar one: it is the Atonement, the doctrine that Christ's suffering redeemed mankind. If much of the poem seems tangential or irrelevant to this theme, that is because Thomas, as we have had occasion to note, thought of the Christian legend only as a leading instance of the natural cycle; the Christian iconography that dominates the poem dramatizes the dialectic of nature and its spiritual implications, but it is not their definitive embodiment.

III

W. S. Merwin, in his essay "The Religious Poet," illustrates Thomas' use of mythic and religious material by showing that "A Winter's Tale" closely resembles legends about midwinter rebirth found in primitive cultures. Merwin's version of the hypothetical legend which might have served as the source of the poem could hardly be improved upon.

Once in the dead of winter, in the middle of the night, a man who lived alone in a house in the woods saw outside a beautiful she-bird, and all around her it was spring. He ran from the house to find her; she flew ahead of him, and all night he ran and at last she came down and he came to where she was; she put her wings over him and the spring faded back to winter; then she rose and vanished, and when spring came and the snow melted they found his body lying on a hill-top.[13]

Though there are some differences between the action of the poem and this narrative, they do not interfere with Merwin's point that "A Winter's Tale" is recognizable as a counterpart of a ceremonial celebrating or anticipating the return of spring.

The prayer Thomas' man says is curious, for it asks for deliverance through annihilation as well as union, thus recognizing the nature of what is to come. The passage from loneliness to love is also a passage from life to death and from awareness to oblivion. As the apparition of the bird and the moment of communion approach, the long, winding sentences of the verse give way to a curt, arbitrary, declarative style in the present tense:

> The wizened
> Stream with bells and baying water bounds. The dew rings
> On the gristed leaves and the long gone glistening
> Parish of snow. The carved mouths in the rock are wind
> swept strings.
> Time sings through the intricately dead snow drop. Listen.

This language of magic is used to describe the two miraculous transformations of nature and reality, the metamorphoses of winter into spring. With the pursuit, the long, syntactically obscure sentences return, culminating in one that simply lists the realities, actual and potential, of the man's situation:

> The sky, the bird, the bride,
> The cloud, the need, the planted stars, the joy beyond
> The fields of seed. . . .

His union with the bird comes as a second stage of the spell which first brought her to him, for the image of the mysteriously opening door reappears, with the significant variation that "the dark door" of his house has now become the metaphoric "door of his death." The action for which this metaphor stands is the descent of the bird. With it is resumed the present-tense language of magical transformation; and the spell of the dancers, the minstrel, and the nightingale that came to disguise the reality of the winter season now disappears. Concurrently with this second transformation, the man and the bird unite, an event expressed in dense imagery involving apotheosis, sexual congress, and annihilation, a merging of incompatibles. In passing from earth to heaven, the man is something burning in water, the bride is "woman breasted" and "heaven headed"; yet the whirlpool of desire is "the spun bud of the world," and the lover who has sought nonexistence has found a new existence in "flowering," in joining the unconscious growth of nature.

The experience of death that the poem dramatizes is the moment of interchange between Thomas' biological cycles; it is like the point where the apexes of two cones meet: mortal life is narrowed to extinction before it passes into the widening possibilities of union with nature. Speaking of the death which is rebirth in *18 Poems,* Thomas said, "I dreamed my genesis in sweat of death." But the redemptive nightmare of *18 Poems* has obviously assumed new qualities in "A Winter's Tale." Invested with the atmosphere of a fairy tale, provided with graceful dramatic action like that of a ballet and with a subtle and sophisticated verse rhythm, it is now more like the vision of a spell than an illusion generated by subconscious conflicts. This world is not the narrow one of *18 Poems,* but one of abundant sensations, clearly realized landscapes, and a whole bestiary of objective creatures. The notions of the continuity of life and the passage from material into spiritual reality, instead of being pressed home through chains of unwavering parallel statements, as they are in *18 Poems,* are elaborated into a silver-gray fantasy employing a variety of rhetorical, dramatic, and narrative resources.

Different as they are, "A Winter's Tale" and "The Ballad of

the Long-Legged Bait" betray a common origin in Thomas' imagination. The central action in each proceeds from sexual attraction between a human being and an animal; the bait is "wanting flesh," the she-bird becomes a "wanting centre." Like the rites of bestiality found in primitive religions, these actions demonstrate, through the sexual congress of different species, the unity of nature. In both poems the union is, for the human being, an act of submission to suffering in an alien environment, "the white/Inhuman cradle" of the she-bird's nest in the snow, or the "cruel bed" of the sea. In fact, the fate the lover in "A Winter's Tale" desires, as it is described in the last two stanzas, is precisely that of the bait: immersion and annihilation in "the bride bed of love" as a prologue to a new life.

There are other parallels in imagery and striking resemblances between the general conditions of the two poems. The fields of "A Winter's Tale" are the same "floating fields" that cover the water in "The Ballad of the Long-Legged Bait," for their merging with the sea is implied in a number of images. The she-bird appears "rayed like a burning bride" before the man begins his pursuit, just as the fishes are "rayed in blood" when the bait is thrown to them. The bread that appears in "The Ballad" as a metaphoric equivalent for the bait, something cast on the water for the fish, also appears in "A Winter's Tale"; and it is also, after several odd transformations, brought to the water. It is first associated with the snow, probably because both are white, in "pure as the drifting bread"; then with the ground, which has been whitened by the snow; but, since the "bread of the ground" is afloat on the water, the combinations of "drifting bread" and "fields of the bread of water" all turn in the direction of the "long-legged bread" of "The Ballad." These turns and twists of metaphor, no doubt worked out through elaborate processes of revision, seem to belong to a single vein of thought.

After an argument for the relationship of the two poems has been made in this way, it is also necessary to take account of the obvious fact that they are, as finished works, radically different. "The Ballad" is jocular, playful, and effervescent in its early and middle passages; and it settles down, at its conclusion, to good-natured resignation. "A Winter's Tale" is solemn, measured, and intense. It is a smooth, cautiously differentiated fabric of verse, almost without seams; but "The Ballad" makes a point of its climaxes and contrasts. These differences reflect the fact that the two poems, in spite of their common features of idiom and imagery, are occupied with different feelings. "The Ballad" is about the resolution of spiritual or psychological conflict; "A Winter's Tale" concerns the passage from one existence to another. The first is about an entry, or, at least, a new entry into life; the second, about an entry into death.

IV

According to Tindall, who had his information directly from Thomas, the subject of "The Ballad of the Long-Legged Bait" is the experience of a young man who sows wild oats and reaps domesticity. Olson interprets the poem as a narrative of salvation through "mortification of the flesh"; the bait symbolizes the fisherman's sensuality; and, in casting her into the sea, he offers a sacrifice in order to bring about a return to innocence and joy. Glauco Cambon also regards the fisherman's action as a sacrifice; the bait is both his sexual partner and his ego and, in fishing with her, he is seeking to exchange the limitations of ordinary perception for the possibilities of mystic vision.[14] Such readings help to fix the shape of the poem, but, as Cambon points out, its details are likely to be misconstrued if they are forced to serve as confirmations of the theme. Transposing them into a set of intellectually encompassable meanings produces results particularly inapposite to the poem itself. Its paradoxes and grotesqueness are not to be reduced to rational ideas but are to be confronted as examples of what the real world discloses to the vision of the mystic. Such inventions as "She nipped and dived in the nick of love. . . ." ". . . the sensual ruins make/Seasons over the liquid world" and "The country tide is cobbled with waves" are complexities generated by the effort to take full account of the incongruities of a dialectic universe.

None of the parallels and analogues that might be set beside the poem quite correspond to it or clarify it. Horace Gregory has mentioned De la Mare's poem, "The Old Angler," which,

like Wilde's tale, "The Fisherman and His Soul," and the fishing
legends they resemble, represent the female figure as the catch,
not the bait.[15] Thomas' fantasies, "In the Direction of the Beginning," and "An Adventure From a Work in Progress,"
share much of the action and imagery of the poem, as Tindall
has pointed out; and they also exemplify, somewhat less obscu-
rely, the method it employs—that of psychological allegory.
Its actions and details are counterparts of emotions and spiritual experiences. This is the real justification for the comparisons
with Rimbaud's *Bateau ivre* and with Shelley's *Alastor* which
have been suggested. Shelley's hero clearly explains the function
of the setting in these voyages of self-discovery:

> Thy darksome stillness,
> Thy dazzling waves, thy loud and hollow gulfs,
> Thy searchless fountain, and invisible course
> Have each their type in me. . . .[16]

Actuality serves as the raw material of this symbolism; elements
drawn from it are shifted and reshaped to represent psychological processes which can, as in *Bateau ivre,* be exceptionally
arbitrary and original. Cambon, in fact, finds that the most
significant resemblance between Thomas' poem and that of
Rimbaud is the *dérèglement* of their vision.

The "Ballad's" sequence of events is fairly clear. The fisherman leaves his friendly town, which sees him off with its best
wishes; and he begins to fish with his startling "long-
legged bait," "A girl alive with his hooks through her lips." A
storm arises, and the creatures of the sea respond to the bait
in an upheaval of energy involving sexual fulfillment, a purgation of lust and the death of the girl. The fisherman then reels in
his bait and finds attached to her a variety of matters including
his forefathers, who pronounce a curse upon time; a countryside
which expands over the water until it reveals his town and
himself, "lost," standing in the doorway of his house, carrying
the bait, which is now his heart, in his hand. The chief issues
involved in this fantasy are suggested, I believe, by the eccentric
behavior of the anchor. At the beginning of the voyage in the
"Ballad," and also in "An Adventure From a Work in Progress,"

the anchor leaps into the sky and flies like a bird; at the end of the poem, when the fisherman has been surrounded by his town, it "dives through the floors of a church," responding to the force of gravity. The voyage then, is an excursion of the imagination which cancels the most familiar conditions of actuality; its conclusion is a return to the conventional and the prosaic.

The bait is identified at the end of the poem as the fisherman's heart; unlike the imagination-created women in "The Hunchback in the Park" and in "The Mouse and the Woman," and unlike the tall woman in "An Adventure From a Work in Progress," she is not the object of the poet's desire; she is an idealized projection of himself, corresponding to the Jungian *anima*. Her immersion in the fertile and teeming sea, the commotion created among the sea creatures, and the "Huge weddings in the waves" are episodes of his mental or spiritual life. For in "An Adventure," it is the narrator's boat which creates this disturbance, and in the "Ballad," the boat pulled about by the sporting bait is "in the burn of my blood." But this consummation has been both a sacrifice and a purgation; the bait has been "kissed dead," and with her also disappear the figures of a tempter, Lucifer and Venus.

The imagery testifies to the complicated nature of this event. In it the bait has played the part of a "bride" at a "wedding," a point of view prepared by the earlier comparison of the bells in the buoys to cathedral chimes; but her "cruel bed" is also a "graveyard in the water." The duality of erotic desire is reflected by the fact that its death is celebrated by the singing of the nightingale and by the howling of the hyena, and that the dead girl is now both "Valley and sahara in a shell." But it has been a willing sacrifice, like bread thrown to birds, and a prelude to reform and regeneration.

The voyage in "An Adventure From a Work in Progress" ends in escape rather than reform. In the story, the hero, after a landfall on an oddly animate island—an erotic landscape resembling the islands in "The Map of Love"—pursues a tall woman who moves unattainably before him. This figure, who is central in the story, appears in the "Ballad" as a minor element in the image of the tempter exhibiting dreams of "Mast-high moon-white women naked." The eruption of desire in "An Adventure" is accompanied by an obscure phenomenon called the falling of time when "the oaks were felled in the acorn and the lizards laid in the shell." This is clearly the same event as the killing of time urged by the old man in the "Ballad": "The oak is felled in the acorn/And the hawk in the egg kills the wren." When it occurs in "An Adventure," all the ordinary relationships of nature are disrupted, and death, violence, and chaos break out. The forefathers in the "Ballad" are warning that this will be the consequence of the fisherman's sin, but the order of nature is not destroyed; for the sin is counterbalanced when the voyage ends in a resolution.

Whatever the catch may be, there is no doubt that the bait sacrificed for it involves an escape from temptation. Amid the good-natured repetitions of "Always goodbye" and "Always goodluck," there are references to the decline of Venus and Lucifer and the remark that "the flesh is cast." As the catch is made, "The statues of great rain stand still," a reference unintelligible, I believe, except in the light of the fact that in "An Adventure," the hero is nearly buried by an avalanche of statues —"monuments of the dark mud"—that fall upon him from a mountainside during a storm. In the "Ballad," however, the vengeance of the past seems to be withheld; the past itself is brought aboard on the fisherman's hook as "The long dead bite!"

The resurrected dead prove to be a desiccated and cheerless lot. However, they are soon followed by the countryside and by the town which emerge from the water, stuck fast to and interwoven with the body of the girl. The gradual expansion of this landscape over the waves is both the suppression of the wild voyage by the familiar sights of orchards and hayricks, and the return of the prodigal. Thus, the imagination comes home at last to a narrow provincial domain in a conclusion reminiscent of the loss of imaginative power described in "Poem in October" and "Fern Hill." The imagery on which the poem ends turns out to be a counterpart of the Freudian view of the mind; above, on the conscious level, are the comfortable and familiar villages, but they merely float above the "moon-chained and water-wound/Metropolis of fishes," a realm of lost desires ordered by its own mysterious forces whose sounds can be heard on the land.

The parallel of "An Adventure from a Work in Progress"

brings a necessary but neglected emphasis to the significant final line of the poem. When the woman of "An Adventure" is captured, she undergoes a number of hideous metamorphoses, growing younger and smaller until she turns into a little sea monster which spits a "white pool" into the hero's hand. In the "Ballad," fulfillment also results in a dwindling, the dwindling of desire, so that the bait, once a full-sized woman, can ultimately be held in the fisherman's hand. In "An Adventure" sin results in horror; in the "Ballad," however, it is cancelled as the passions that produced it are reduced and controlled.

V

In his comments on "Vision and Prayer," Tindall, whose personal relations with Thomas had not impressed him with the poet's piety, suggests that the religious conversion it describes is a metaphor for something else. The doctrines of martyrdom and redemption found in the poem function as the Christian myths usually do in Thomas: they are representatives of his general pantheism. Like the symbols which appear in the poem that Christianity has in common with other religions (such as darkness, light, birth, and sacrifice), they are used to express a personal fervor. In the first section the poet has a vision that the child being born in the next room is a Christ or Messiah who will bring deliverance. The prayer of the second section asks that fallen humanity be spared this redemption (as Francis Thompson does in "The Hound of Heaven,") but its final stanza is an ecstatic capitulation to it. Each of the two sections embodies a conflict between the desire to follow the easy way to perdition and a call to the arduous glories of salvation.

The poem is Thomas' climactic treatment of a subject that is exceptionally persistent in his work—the birth of a holy child. A birth that is an affliction on the material level, but a deliverance on the spiritual one is also the subject of "Before I knocked," of "If my head hurt a hair's foot," and of "A saint about to fall." "Vision and Prayer" echoes these parturition poems, suggesting that all emerge from the core of thought generated by the birth of Llewelyn. The last three have in common the same squalid setting: a "loud room" or an "odd room" or a "birth bloody room" in a "split house" or "an old mud hatch." The child lies in his mother's womb like an iron stranger, and the familiar image of the creative explosion reappears in the imagery of disastrous impact associated with his birth. The leveling of the "wren-bone wall" is echoed in the idea that the saint about to fall would bring "the unwinding . . . of the woven wall/Of his father's house." The quixotic notion that the birth can be undone appears in both "Vision and Prayer" and "If my head hurt a hair's foot."

In "Vision and Prayer," as in the earlier poems, the redemptive birth involves a sacrifice; for the environment the child is born into is unpropitious. Sacrifice is represented symbolically by the impressive image of the expurgatory burning of the child, an action which, as we have noted, climaxes the 1936 short story, "The Burning Baby," and then, apparently in response to actual events of the war, is developed in "A Refusal to Mourn" and in "Ceremony After a Fire Raid." In "Vision and Prayer," however, the child does not suffer from the flames; a sun-deity swaddled in his element, he brings fire to illuminate the spiritual darkness of the earth. He is greeted, not by baptism, but by "dark alone/Blessing"; and the poet, "Casting to-morrow like a thorn," foresees that his life will be hard. But the holy fire quickly mounts to an irresistible intensity of purgation, bringing down the wall of separation between the child and the poet and exposing the father to the terror of "the first dawn/Furied by his stream." As a result, in the fifth stanza, he confronts a primordial, fragmented universe of sea, cloud, dust, and flame, all swirling in elemental energy. The section then closes in a series of exclamations acknowledging the interweaving of origins and endings in the timelessness of the visionary's universe. What is apostrophized in

> O spiral of ascension
>   From the vultured urn
>   Of the morning
>   Of man. . . .

is the mounting cycle of life, originating in a birth that includes (as the allusion to the "ascension" of Jesus implies) death. The "woundward flight" of the young and the battle of the last stanza are all "The world winding home" through a life of suffering to a death of deliverance. In the last two lines, the poet, who has been witnessing the agony of the birth, fixes himself into this pattern as laconically as possible. In the birth of the child, he sees his death.

The long opening sentence of the second section prays, paradoxically, that the birth of the child and the deliverance it promises may be averted. Two of the elements in the setting of this prayer assert the identity of life and death forces in the natural cycle; "the lost" are in "the swinish plains of carrion," and these recall a passage from one of the manuscript poems mentioned earlier describing a place of lechery. Also, the carrion borne by the scavenging birds is seen as potentially life-giving, for it is "green," and "like pollen."

The first sentence asks that the child may return to the womb. The second asks that the lost not be redeemed, and the image of sleep as a metaphoric equivalent for lack of faith, familiar from *18 Poems*, recurs here, as the poet prays that the child

> Rock
> Awake
> No heart bone
> But let it break. . . .

To these sinners, existence will seem a "night forever falling," but this appearance of the world is familiar to "the legion/ Of sleepers," whose indifference does not dull their intellectual capacities, for they know the labyrinths of perdition, and so are "charting sleepers." Their desire to sleep is personified as "common lazarus," one subject to resurrection, but, in this case, unwilling to experience it. Two lines that end one stanza and begin the next give the reasons for this prayer: "For the country of death is the heart's size/And the star of the lost the shape of the eyes." Man is naturally fallen, and spiritual death and loss are appropriate to him. The following sentence closes the prayer proper by asking that the child be reduced to human stature by being stripped of his divinity. But the "amen" is followed by exclamations indicating an involuntary and intense conversion that is conveyed through imagery of light, heat, and annihilation.

The most conspicuous feature of the poem, the revival of the seventeenth-century device of the shaped poem, naturally arouses interest. Traditionally, these shapes are suggestive of objects, as in George Herbert's "The Altar" and "Easter Wings"; and the shapes of the stanzas in "Vision and Prayer" may be performing this function. Critics have suggested that the stanzas of Section 1 represent diamonds or lozenges or the opening womb, and that those of Section 2 are like hourglasses, hatchets, flagons, and wings. However, less concrete equivalents may be more satisfactory. The shape of the stanza in Section 1 seems to reflect the idea of "opening" which prevails in it, both in relation to birth and to spiritual awakening. In Section 2, the convergence of forces or reversal suggested by the stanza form corresponds with the conflict of impulses which is the subject. It also reflects (more particularly by its rhythm), the withholding, followed by the yielding of assent.

Nearly as striking as the shapes themselves are the individual words they emphasize by isolating them at the ends or in the middle of stanzas. A subtle suggestiveness is achieved by placing "Die" at the end of the first section, by using "No" as the narrow hinge of the penultimate stanza, and by "I" as the axis-like connective between the parts of the last one.

CHAPTER 8

Stories and Plays

I

Thomas was as prolific a writer of prose as of verse. He published the first of his short stories, "After the Fair," in March, 1934,
less than a year after his earliest poems had appeared; and he
continued to write prose until his death. In addition to his
numerous short stories, the uncompleted novel, *Adventures in
the Skin Trade*, three prose dramas, the radio play, *Under
Milk Wood*, and the two film scripts, *The Doctor and the Devils*
and *The Beach at Falesá*, he wrote a number of book reviews,
radio talks, and descriptive essays, many of them collected in
the posthumous volume, *Quite Early One Morning*.[1]

Thomas' fiction may be divided sharply into two classifi-
cations: vigorous fantasies in poetic style, a genre he discon-
tinued after 1939; and straightforward, objective narratives.
Until 1939 he seems to have thought of the short prose narrative
as an alternate poetic form—as a vehicle for recording the
action of the imagination in reshaping objective reality according to private desire. Almost every story of this period (the
exceptions being "After the Fair" and "The Tree") perceives
actuality through the screen of an irrational mind. The main
characters are madmen, simpletons, fanatics, lechers, and poets
in love: people enslaved by the dictates of feeling. Their stories
are narrated in a heavily poetic prose reflecting the confusion
of actual and imaginary experiences which constitutes their
reality, so that the material and psychological intersect without
a joint, forming a strange new area of being. For example, as
Mr. Davies, the deluded rector of "The Holy Six," is washing
the feet of his six colleagues, believing that he is performing a
holy deed, we are told that "light brought the inner world to
pass," that his misconception was transformed into actuality.

Some of the stories seem transitional in style, enabling the reader to witness these transformations as an outsider. In "The Dress," the fleeing madman, who yearns for a chance to sleep, thinks of sleep as personified by another object of desire—a girl. When he breaks into the cottage where the young housewife is sitting, he follows the logic of his delusion, mistakes her for sleep, and puts his head in her lap.

The setting of most of these stories is the seaside Welsh town wickedly called Llareggub (to be read backwards), also the scene of *Under Milk Wood,* with its neighboring countryside, including a valley named after Jarvis, a lecherous nineteenth-century landlord, some farms, and a mountain called Cader Peak. Among the inhabitants of this region are young men obsessed by unfulfilled love, as in "The Mouse and the Woman" and "The Orchards"; clergymen crazed by lust, as in "The Holy Six" and "The Burning Baby"; wise men or women who teach some cabalistic magic art, as in "The Tree," "The Map of Love," "The School for Witches," and "The Lemon"; and enigmatic girls who rise from the sea or the soil as in "The Mouse and the Woman" and "A Prospect of the Sea." The fancies of these people, narrated in a manner rendering them indistinguishable from objective reality, fill the town and the countryside with visions, supernatural forces, and fantastic episodes recalling the world of fairy tale and of folklore. People and objects are whisked into new shapes, small and intimate experiences are magnified until they embody fundamental realities—"creation screaming in the steam of the kettle"—and the order of nature is constantly subject to disruption. In this milieu the anomalous is the ordinary; at the end of "Prologue to an Adventure," for example, the barroom where the two friends are standing runs down the drains of the town into the sea.

In one of his letters to Vernon Watkins, Thomas observes that the reader of verse needs an occasional rest but that the poet ought not to give it to him; this sustained intensity is more natural to poetry than to prose. In applying this principle to his stories, Thomas produced complex, involuted narratives with rich surfaces of language and imagery. At first impression they have no depths; but analysis shows that the order of imagination operating in them is the one which produced Thomas' poetry. His stories, unlike his earliest poems, deal with recognizable people and places; but they invest them with the same mythic atmosphere found in the poems. As we have already observed, there are numerous and detailed affinities between the poems and these early, fantastic stories. Common themes, the burning of a child, the "falling" of time, the unity of life, and the verbal capacities of nature provide subjects for both, and are also reflected in rhetorical details. But the most general resemblance is an awareness of the cosmic import of small events, a tendency to develop the significance of experiences by referring them to the absolute limits of the continuum of which they are a part. The lust of Rhys Rhys in "The Burning Baby" culminates in incest and in the murder of his child; the desire of the poet in "The Mouse and the Woman" raises a beautiful woman for him on the seashore; the vision of heaven the boy sees from the top of his ladder in "A Prospect of the Sea" is an endless Eden stretching to meet itself above and below.

II

In "The Tree," which first appeared in the *Adelphi* in December, 1934, within a week of the publication of *18 Poems,* the style typical of Thomas' fantastic stories is still at an early stage of its development, so that it is possible to distinguish actual events from the delusions going on in the minds of the characters. The story also provides a convenient dramatization of the creative process at work in these stories. The gardener transmits his obsession to the boy; the boy, at the end of the story, tries to transform it into actuality. In writing his fantastic stories, Thomas, the narrator, acted the part of the boy. Borrowing delusions from his characters, Thomas produced in the narrative itself a version of reality corresponding to the delusions.

The gardener in the story is a naïve religious who, by one of those primitive metaphorical associations familiar to us from Thomas' poems, takes all trees as counterparts of the "tree" of the cross. As he tells the boy the story of Jesus, the child fixes on the elder tree in the garden as the scene of the crucifixion. When he is let into the locked tower as a Christmas

gift, the boy is bitterly disappointed to find it empty; but he
associates the Jarvis hills, which are visible through the
window, with Bethlehem; for they, like Bethlehem, are toward
the east. The idiot standing under the tree in the garden, exposed
to the wind and rain, has already had Christlike intimations of
his destiny when the boy finds him in the morning. And when
the boy learns that he has come from the eastern hills that he
has mistaken for Bethlehem, he fits the tree, the hills, and the
idiot into the pattern described by the gardener, and sets about
making the story of Jesus a reality. As the story closes, he has
put the idiot against the tree and is crucifying him on it. The
ultimate point of the story is the idiot's acceptance of his suffering; in the final scene the ignorant piety of the gardener is being
transformed, through the imagination of the child and the love
and humility of the idiot, into a reality.

The narrative style blending actual and imagined worlds
appears for the first time in "The Visitor," whose main character,
as he approaches death, perceives the continuity between the
living and dead aspects of the cosmos. Because we know the
actual world which is the background of his delusion, we can
see that the first part of the narrative has a double structure; and
we can easily separate Peter's delusions from external reality.
His idea that the sheets are shrouds, that his heart is a clock
ticking, and that he lacks feelings because he is dead are simply
misinterpretations of sensory clues. Only occasionally does his
mind drift into clear hallucination, as when he thinks he is look-
ing down at his own dead face in the coffin. Otherwise his
thoughts are perfectly intelligible; he recalls that his first wife
died seven years earlier in childbirth, and the guilt he experiences is expressed in a remarkable metaphor: "He felt his
body turn to vapour, and men who had been light as air walked,
metal-hooved, through and beyond him."

In the second part of the story, however, we enter fully
into Peter's dying delirium and the basis of fact offered by the
external world fades away. In a region of pure fantasy, we are
unable, like Peter himself, to distinguish the imaginary from the
real or even to detect the moment of division between life and
death. In his delirium, Callaghan, the visitor Peter has been expecting, comes and carries him away into a realm of essential

being where the pulsations of alternate growth and destruction are perfectly visible in a stripped, transparent landscape. Here a new prose style, the one Thomas adopts as a means of objectifying mystical perception, presents itself. More descriptive than narrative, it is full of grotesque, clearly realized images. Sometimes rhapsodic, sometimes strangely matter of fact, it seeks to capture the disruption imposed upon nature by hallucinatory vision. As in the poems, metaphor ceases to compare, and equates instead, so that "the flowers shot out of the dead," and "the light of the moon . . . pulled the moles and badgers out of their winter."

The journey ends when Peter, suddenly returned to his sickbed again, feels restored to his body and speaks to his wife. But she does not hear him, and he does not realize he is dead until she pulls the sheet over his face. Just as he had the delusion, when he was living, that he was dead, so at the end Peter has the delusion, when he is dead, that he is alive. The division between the two states is slight, and disembodied vitality persists so powerfully that moving from the aspect of being we call life to the one we call death hardly matters to it. As one of the poems concludes, "The heart is sensual, though five eyes break."

In "The Visitor," Peter experiences actual and imaginary realms at different times; the two meet only at the boundary between them, where their edges are not clear. But in the further development of his narrative style, Thomas presented situations where imagined and actual events are superimposed upon one another as single experiences. Two closely related short stories published in 1936, "The Orchards" and "The Mouse and the Woman," illustrate this. Both have the same theme as "The Hunchback in the Park": the creation of an imaginary woman by a mind obsessed by the need for love. And both are tragedies of delusion, for they show that the dreamer is pitifully exposed to the demands of the actual world.

The woman loved by Marlais, the poet of "The Orchards," comes to him in a dream in the form of a scarecrow who stands, with her sister, in a landscape of burning orchards. When he wakes up, the memory of this dream persists and distracts him from his writing. Oppressed by the disparity between the passion of his dream thoughts and the dullness of the town outside his window, Marlais makes an effort of the imagination which leads him to mystic perception. What follows is perhaps Thomas' most complete description of mystic vision. The distinction between objective and subjective is canceled: "There was dust in his eyes; there were eyes in the grains of dust. . . ." Individual things seem part of greater wholes, saturated with absolute significance: "His hand before him was five-fingered life." Opposites are reconciled: "It is all one, the loud voice and the still voice striking a common silence. . . ." Intoxicated with the feeling that he commands both spiritual and actual realms, so that he is "man among ghosts, and ghost in clover," Marlais now "moved for the last answer."

A second sleep shows him that the landscape of his dream and the woman he loves are still there; and when he wakes he goes out of the town to find it. The second half of the story, like that of "The Visitor," is the journey of a mental traveler; but Marlais travels on the ground, not in the air, as Peter does. And his imagined world is spread over the real countryside, whose objective features emerge, like peaks rising out of the clouds of his thoughts. The Whippet valley, a part of the real countryside which has been destroyed by mining, is succeeded by a wood whose trees are said to spring from the legend of the Fall. As his walk continues, Marlais enters the realm of myth and becomes a myth himself; when he has penetrated into this imaginary world, he finds the orchards of his dream and the girl in it. An objective observer would probably say that Marlais had been invited to have a picnic tea with an ordinary girl; for the tablecloth, cups, and bread she produces are real enough. But, as Marlais views the scene, the conditions of his dream impose themselves upon this objective reality, and the scene is transformed to correspond with it. The orchards break into fire; the girl is changed into a scarecrow and calls up her sister, as in the dream; and Marlais has his desire.

But we have been warned at the beginning that Marlais' passion was "a story more terrible than the stories of the reverend madmen in the Black Book of Llareggub," and the conclusion tells us why. The fires of Marlais' dream are put out by "the real world's wind," and it becomes a fact, not a dream.

The imaginative tide of his obsession recedes, leaving him stranded in actuality, kissing a scarecrow, and exposing his madness.

"The Mouse and the Woman" is a more elaborate treatment of the same theme: the betrayal of a poet by his obsession with love. In this story, as in "The Orchards," the hero creates a dream woman, and he shuttles back and forth between a dream world and a waking world that seem equally real. But Thomas has added to the situation a moral aspect represented by the mouse. The story opens with a remarkable description of the madman in the lunatic asylum, and it then moves back in his memory to trace the steps of his alienation. As in "The Orchards," the woman comes to him in a dream, and her memory persists when he is awake until he is caught between reality and delusion; he does not know whether to believe in her existence or not. He creates her by writing about her, ". . . it was upon the block of paper that she was made absolute," thus surrendering to imagination; he then goes out on the beach to find her and bring her to his cottage. This begins the part of the story where hallucination is perfectly superimposed upon actuality. The girl is, of course, pure imagination; but the mouse, which is associated with evil, and the mousehole the hero nails up to keep it away seem representative of objective actuality. Oddly, within this waking dream the hero has nocturnal dreams containing frightening enigmatic symbols. When he strips the girl and becomes her lover, two related events follow: the mouse emerges from its hole; and the notion of original sin enters the consciousness of the lovers as the man tells the girl the story of the Fall. She realizes that he has felt evil in their relationship.

The mouse and what it represents are the seed of destruction in his euphoric delusion; for the woman leaves him. Though he pursues her, she will not have him back. Her rejection of him is marvelously conveyed in the fairy tale episode where he lights upon her hand, like an insect, pleads with her, and is crushed as she closes her hand over him. Since he has created her by thought, he can kill her by thought. He writes "The woman died" on his writing pad, and we are told that "There was dignity in such a murder." He sees her dead body lying on the beach. But the knowledge that "he had failed . . . to hold his miracle" is too much for him, and he becomes the madman who appears at the beginning of the story.

The story goes a step further than "The Orchards," for it explains why the certainty offered by delusion should disappear. The poet's sense of guilt, emerging from within his mind as the mouse emerges from the walls of the house, poisons his dream. His derangements are no longer orderly and joyful, but confused: "The secret of that alchemy that had turned a little revolution of the unsteady senses into a golden moment was lost as a key is lost in the undergrowth." He has regained some contact with the objective world, but he wants to kill the woman. And, in order to do this, he must return to the world of imagination where she exists. In killing her, he also kills the dream she dominates, on which his happiness depends. The mouse, now fully in possession of the kitchen, silently presides over the grief he feels at this self-destruction. Trapped between two systems of reality and unable to commit himself to either, the poet can only howl at life from behind the bars of the asylum.

In four stories published in 1937 and 1938, the hallucinatory technique advances so far that it is no longer possible—or desirable—to disentangle imagined from actual episodes. External reality responds flexibly to the thoughts and feelings of the characters, so that the narrative amounts to a psychological allegory. This genre, it will be recalled, is the one to which "Ballad of the Long-Legged Bait" belongs, and two of the four stories now under discussion are so closely related to this poem that they seem to be prose sketches for it. The member of this group closest to the earlier stories is "A Prospect of the Sea." It has the same elements as "The Orchards" and "The Mouse and the Woman": a girl who is encountered at the seashore, and who disappears, and a delirious shuttling back and forth between different orders of reality.

In "A Prospect of the Sea," the boy begins by enjoying the summer day and then makes up a story about a drowned princess; but this level of thought is intersected by another—the appearance of a country girl who confronts him in the actual landscape. This siren figure both tempts and terrifies him, for she has the power to make the world swell and shrink. His fantasies of death and disfigurement alternate with the actual events of her erotic advances. As evening comes, he yields himself to another daydream, a mystic's vision of power, piercing sight, and multiplied Edens. But the girl calls him into an actual world that is now strangely insubstantial: ". . . she could make a long crystal of each tree, and turn the house wood into gauze." She leads him on a race through a mystically disrupted realm; and then, in the morning, in spite of his agonized protests, she walks into the sea and disappears. As he turns to walk inland, he confronts the elements of the Noah story: an old man building a boat, the beginning of rainfall, and a stream of animals entering the door. Apparently, then, the episodes of the story belong to the corrupt time God had determined to end by means of the Flood.

But "A Prospect of the Sea" is an innocent pastoral in comparison with "Prologue to an Adventure," a chronicle of town sin, a subject that offers a far richer opportunity for Thomas' grotesque metaphoric energies than the country scenes of the earlier stories. There is little action. The speaker wanders through the streets and, with an acquaintance named Daniel Dom (a variant of the name "Domdaniel" appearing in one of Thomas' unpublished poems),[2] visits two bars; then, as in "A Prospect of the Sea," destructive water comes as the scene is immersed by waves.

The interest of this story lies in the remarkable play of scenes and imagery conveying the feverish atmosphere of a night on the town. "Now in the shape of a bald girl smiling, a wailing wanton with handcuffs for earrings, or the lean girls that live on pickings, now in ragged women with a muckrake curtseying in the slime, the tempter of angels whispered over my shoulder." As the speaker says, there is "more than man's meaning" in this torrent of fearsome, Hieronymus Boschlike visions, for holiness is caught up and debased in it. "I have the God of Israel in the image of a painted boy, and Lucifer, in a woman's shirt, pisses from a window in Damaroid Alley."

The two scenes in the bars are incoherent jumbles of fleeing images, glimpses of transcendental visions, and striking expressionistic effects. They look backward in technique and subject to the Circe scene of Joyce's *Ulysses* and forward to Thomas' *Doctor and the Devils* for their atmosphere of pinched debauchery. The speaker and his friend aspire for a moment to reach out of this welter of temptresses, oppressed children, and indifferent city streets to some heavenly goal, but they come instead to a new bar where, after joining the corrupt festivities, they turn to the window and witness the coming of the deluge. There are no alternate realms of reality in this story. It is all an inescapable mental reality, consisting entirely of representations of the desires, fears, suspicions, and other emotions of the narrator; for, as his visions tell him, "We are all metaphors of the sound of shape, of the shape of sound, break us we take another shape."

"In the Direction of the Beginning" and "An Adventure from a Work in Progress" are mythlike tales written in a hallucinatory style. The first, a short account of the creation, tells of the appearance of figures resembling Adam and Eve. Its enchanted, visionary prose presents a dizzying succession of images referring fleetingly to various seasons, ages, and episodes of history and legend. There is almost no physical action; the Fall is suggested as the man becomes entrapped by the woman's siren spell and as his obsession with her is projected through imagery showing that he feels her to be personified in every detail of the universe. The same obsession appears in "An Adventure from a Work in Progress," an account of a man pursuing a shadowy woman through a strangely active archipelago where awesome cataclysms endanger him. At the climax of the story the woman merges with the mountain, just as the Eve in "In the Direction of the Beginning" merges with the soil. When the hero ultimately catches her, she undergoes a series of startling metamorphoses and shrinks to a tiny monster in the palm of his hand. After being thus betrayed by his obsession, like the lovers in "The Orchards" and "The Mouse and the Woman," the hero returns from the imaginary world to the actual one, and sails away on "the common sea."

The "revolving islands and elastic hills" of this story show that it takes place in the realm that is more fully described in "The Map of Love." In the latter, the stages of sexual initiation are represented by a bewitched landscape; a curious animated map or model of this region exhibits its vital sexual properties, so that the children to whom it is being displayed blush at "the copulation in the second mud." The libido-charged landscape represented by the map is the world as it presents itself to the heroes of the last two stories, who find the women they love embodied in cliffs, seas, and mountains. The children in "The Map of Love" are guided by Sam Rib, who is named for the origin of love, and are encouraged by the spirit of their lecherous Great-Uncle Jarvis, who speaks to them from the fields where he has lain with ten different mistresses. But they never succeed in swimming up the river to the island of the first beasts of love. Apparently, they are too shy, too lacking in lust; mere "synthetic prodigals" of Sam Rib's laboratory, they are unable to share the dangerous vitality of nature.

Four of the stories of this period form a separate subgroup; "The Enemies," "The Holy Six," "The Burning Baby," and "The School for Witches" are all about the fictional town of Llareggub, and all are told in a narrative style that presents much objective material. Thomas has created a distinctive comic world in these stories, a world of lecherous, hypocritical clergymen and of submissive girls tumbling over an enchanted Welsh landscape into situations appropriate to myths and fairy tales. In "The Enemies," Mr. Davies, the doddering rector of Llareggub, wanders onto the farm of Mr. and Mrs. Owen. The farmer and his wife are a strong pagan pair in tune with the fertility of the soil; and they feel pity for the poor rector who comes to them tired and bleeding, having been betrayed by the countryside where he has been lost. As they eat dinner in the pantheistic atmosphere of the Owen farm, Mr. Davies is suddenly struck by the inadequacy of his own faith, and he falls to his knees to pray in fear. The story ends: "He stared and he prayed, like an old god beset by his enemies." Thomas is distinguishing between the religion he saw represented in the churches of Wales and the one he saw embodied in "the copulation in the tree . . . the living grease in the soil."

In "The Holy Six," a sequel to "The Enemies," Mr. Davies' adventure is turned into channels that are both comic and more deeply religious. Six of his colleagues receive a letter from Mrs. Owen informing them of Mr. Davies' plight. These six are confirmed lechers. "The holy life was a constant erection to these six gentlemen." Much of the story consists of uproarious descriptions of the visions their evil minds project upon actuality. (An allusion to Peter, the poet of "The Visitor," who lives in the Jarvis valley where the Owen farm is, suggests that Thomas thought of all the Llareggub stories as interrelated, though he makes little effort to establish links among them.) When the Six arrive at the Jarvis valley, they find the countryside alien to them, just as Mr. Davies did; and the opposition between their hypocritical faith and that of the Owen couple is developed as Mrs. Owen sees the truth of things in her crystal ball.

Mr. Davies is brought forward, strangely transformed. He has apparently learned the lesson of the fertile soil, but his newly discovered passions have merged with his religious habits of mind to form a grotesque compound of lust and devotion: "his ghost who laboured . . . leapt out to marry Mary; all-sexed and nothing, intangible hermaphrodite riding the neuter dead, the minister of God in a grey image mounted dead Mary." He performs the service of washing the feet of his colleagues, while the thoughts of each are described, forming a series of remarkable surrealist fantasies. When he has finished this task, Mr. Davies cryptically claims the paternity of the child in Mrs. Owen's womb. Though Mr. Owen smiles at this, it is clear that Mr. Davies is right, for their "ghosts" have consummated a spiritual love in a realm different from that of the love of husband and wife.

Religious hypocrisy and repression are condemned in "The Holy Six" and in "The Enemies" mainly by comic means. But "The Burning Baby" treats this theme with a tragic force approaching grandeur. The spectacle of a child consumed by fire, as we know from his poems, impressed Thomas as the formulation of an ultimate question, for it involved the greatest imaginable suffering inflicted on the greatest imaginable innocence. Rhys Rhys, the vicar, who has been driven to seduce his daughter by an obsessive lust, burns the baby resulting from this union in an expurgatory ritual. The baby, like the devil, he considers "poor flesh," and he burns it to rid the earth of the fruit of the "foul womb" and of the evidence of his own sin. But Thomas, speaking in his own voice, corrects Rhys

Rhys' view and insists upon the spiritual symmetry of nature: "The fruit of the flesh falls with the worm from the tree. Conceiving the worm, the bark crumbles. There lay the poor star of flesh that had dropped, like the bead of a woman's milk, through the nipples of a wormy tree." Though the child is dead, the flames awaken him to a shriek of protest which is significantly taken up by the landscape that witnesses his immolation.

"The Burning Baby" is probably the best-sustained and most carefully constructed of Thomas' early stories. Though it is about derangement, its style, with a few exceptions, is disciplined and objective. The moments when the emotions of the characters take over the story and shape the narration are clearly marked. For example, when Rhys Rhys is delivering his usual sermon, but thinking of his desire for his daughter, he thinks: ". . . the good flesh, the mean flesh, flesh of his daughter, flesh, flesh, the flesh of the voice of thunder howling before the death of man." At the moment of the incestuous union, the disruption of the normal order of feelings is reflected by a disruption of the normal conditions of external reality: "The lashes of her fingers lifted. He saw the ball under the nail." Minor events predict what is to come. Rhys Rhys' son, who he thinks is a changeling, brings in a dead rabbit, cradling it like a baby. The scene arouses Rhys Rhys' terrors, and he takes the dead rabbit away, thus appropriating death. But the changeling witnesses the seduction and the sacrifice of the baby, and he insanely re-enacts them after the others are dead.

"The School for Witches" is another story having a baby as the victim of worship, but this worship is not Christianity, but witchcraft. The cut accidentally inflicted on the black woman's baby at the moment of its birth is a warning that it is entering the "wicked world" of the school for witches where the black arts are taught. Most of the story is devoted to descriptions of the rituals, dances, and covens of the witches, the formalized evil that has risen from the cursed and bedeviled countryside. The doctor, the only lucid character, has bleak meditations as he and the midwife carry the baby back to his house: "What purpose there was in the shape of Cader Peak, in the bouldered breast of the hill and the craters poxing the green-black flesh, was no more than the wind's purpose that willy nilly blew from all corners the odd turfs and stones of an unmoulded world. The grassy rags and bones of the steep hill were . . . whirled together out of the bins of chaos by a winter wind." The baby's cry confirms this sadness, and rouses Mr. Griffiths, who thinks the sound is the scream of a mandrake being uprooted and goes out to investigate. When he finds the baby, it is dead, lying neglected at the door of the house where all the other characters in the story are whirling in the mad dance of the witches' coven.

The regional folklore exploited in "The School for Witches" appears in subtler forms in the other fantastic tales. The fairy lady, the changeling, the devil rolling in a ball on the ground (as the lecherous clergymen do in "The Holy Six"), and the spontaneous metamorphoses of scenes and people all belong to the atmosphere of Welsh mythology. The plot of "The Orchards" and of "The Mouse and the Woman," involving a man who meets and loses a fairy woman, is common in these myths. "The Burning Baby" begins in the manner of a folktale, for the story is offered as a heuristic explanation of the sudden bursting into flame of dry bushes. The presence of these borrowings in the stories suggests that there is a similar element in the poems Thomas was writing at this period. The poems contain a few references to folklore, such as the beliefs concerning the vampire and the mandrake. Thomas' interest in this subject raises the possibility that the mythic awareness we have observed in the poems has its ultimate roots in the legends of Wales.

The poems, it will be recalled, encompass two conceptions of time: the unmoving time of mysticism and the conventional notion of time as a power that changes and destroys. Time is also an important theme in at least four of the imaginative stories, for mystic insights, or disruptions of the natural order, psychological or otherwise, are sometimes announced as disruptions of time. The derangement of the poet in "The Mouse and the Woman" takes the form of a decision that winter must be prevented from spoiling the beauty of the woman who has left him and maddened him with jealousy. He attacks "the old effigy" of time, flinging himself into a chaos of irrational images. There is a similar effect in "The Horse's Ha."

When the undertaker drinks the magic brew intended to resurrect the dead, the movements of the sun and moon are disturbed, and the days pass with mysterious rapidity. One of the dreams of the boy in "A Prospect of the Sea" is a sweeping mystic vision in which he sees through time, relating remote things in a single historic unity. Finally, in "An Adventure from a Work in Progress," the man's capture of the first woman he sees on the islands is accompanied by a phenomenon Thomas calls the falling of time. This event is echoed in "Ballad of the Long-Legged Bait"; it involves a reversal of the development of living things; intense disturbances, including a windstorm, fires, earthquakes; and, in fact, all the elements of chaos. Clearly, the timelessness of the poems is inappropriate to the world of the stories. The reason may be that the stories, unlike the early poems, are about human beings living their earthly lives and that the standard of conventional time is indispensable to them. When mortals seek to evade time, as do the boys in "I see the boys of summer," in order to make love endure or to avoid death, chaos results.

III

Thomas was still working on the last of his fantastic narratives in 1938 when he began to write the realistic stories which were collected in *Portrait of the Artist as a Young Dog*. In March, 1938, he wrote to Watkins that the first of "a series of short, straightforward stories about Swansea" had already been published. This statement must refer to "A Visit to Grandpa's," which appeared in the *New English Weekly* on March 10, 1938. The change in narrative style between these two groups of stories is, of course, a radical one; moreover, it paralleled the much more subtle change in Thomas' poetic style that was going on at about the same time. Many of the casual details of these stories are drawn without change from Thomas' Swansea days, and some of the characters are based on actual people: the aunt in "The Peaches" is Ann Jones, and Dan Jenkyns in "The Fight" is Daniel Jones. In his "Poetic Manifesto," Thomas declared that the title he assigned to the collection was a variant, not of Joyce's title, but of one often given by painters to self-portraits. He admitted that the general influence of *Dubliners* might be felt in his stories, but he added that this was an influence no good writer of short stories could avoid.[3]

The protagonist in all the stories is clearly Thomas himself, though the stories are narrated indifferently in first and third persons and though each presents him at a different age. They are about ordinary experiences: visits with relatives, excursions to the country, adventures with gangs of children, explorations of the town. In some of them the plot is so slight that the story approaches a reminiscence or cluster of impressions. Obviously written with only a loose unity in mind, they have no common theme; but taken as a group, they seem to trace the child's emergence from his domain of imagination and secret pleasures into an adult world where he observes suffering, pathos, and dignity.

Most of the stories are about an observer or witness, one whose experience consists of awakening to the experiences of others. The events are presented in sharp, well-selected impressions. When he is observing a general scene, such as a boy's room or a crowded street, Thomas proceeds by piling up a lively list of the quintessential details or characteristic people. Sometimes his attitude toward people, places, and episodes is affectionate or amused; sometimes he finds grotesque nightmare evocations in them. But he encounters his strongest emotions in moments of solitude when he can hug his general impressions of the external world to himself as personal possessions—while walking down a street late at night, wandering in moody isolation on a noisy beach, or enjoying the atmosphere of an expensive bar.

The first three stories—"The Peaches," "A Visit to Grandpa's" and "Patricia, Edith and Arnold"—set the idyllic existence of a child side by side with the trials of adults. As the grownups suffer, the child remains indifferent or cruel; yet it appears at the end that he has understood and sympathized more than he knew, thus anticipating the ultimate union of the childish and adult points of view. "The Peaches" may be said to have "separateness" as an identifiable theme. Mrs. Williams, who brings her son for a holiday at the farm, is too superior to stay a moment longer than necessary, and refuses the precious canned peaches that have been saved for her visit. Jim curses her snobbery, but he cannot keep himself from drinking up the profits of the farm and distressing his wife. Gwilym, the son, who closely resembles the religious gardener in "The Tree," is occupied with a vision of himself as a preacher, and makes the barn a church for his pretended sermons. To these mutually uncommunicating attitudes toward life is added that of the boys who are busy with their games of wild Indian and indifferent to the concerns of the adults. But even here a division occurs when Jack Williams betrays his playmate by telling his mother an incriminating mixture of truth and falsehood about his treatment at the farm, and is taken away. At the end of "The Peaches," the boy waves his handkerchief at his departing betrayer, innocent that any wrong has been done to him, or to his aunt and uncle.

But in "Patricia, Edith and Arnold," the child, at first cruelly indifferent to the pain felt by the two maidservants who have learned that the same young man has been walking out with both of them, gains some insight into adult sorrows. The story begins with a chaos of irreconcilable interests: the absorption of the girls in their love triangle, and the rambunctious joy of the child who is all-conquering in his imaginary play world. But as the painful comedy of Arnold's entrapment is played out, the boy, uncomfortably cold and wet, feels his own distress and unconsciously comes to sympathize with Patricia. Returning to the shelter to retrieve his cap, he sees Arnold reading the letters he has written to the other girl, but he mercifully spares Patricia this knowledge. And his own experience of pain, a minor counterpart of the adult pain Paticia has suffered, comes when he thaws his cold hands at the fire. Patricia's final remark, "Now we've all had a good cry today," formulates both the similarity of their trials and their capacity to endure them.

Cruel jokes, of the sort that life has played on Arnold, occur in some of the other stories. In "Just Like Little Dogs," the brothers exchange partners with each other in the middle of an evening of casual love. As a result, when the women become pregnant, it is not clear which brother is the father of their respective children. The two forced but loveless marriages take place, and now the two fathers spend their evenings in the street, standing hopelessly in the cold night air. In "Old Garbo," the neighbors take up a collection for Mrs. Prothero, whose daughter is supposed to have died in childbirth; after Mrs. Prothero has drunk up the money, it is learned that the daughter has survived. The mother, ashamed at having taken the money under false pretenses, jumps into the river.

It is significant that in each of these stories the anecdotal nucleus is subordinated to the vehicle which conveys it. The impressive element of "Just Like Little Dogs" is the spectacle of the young men sheltering aimlessly from the night under the railway arch; they have no place more interesting to go and nothing more interesting to do. "Old Garbo" is, in reality, a story of initiation; the young reporter, eager to share the knowledge and maturity of the older one, follows him into the haunts where Mrs. Prothero's comic tragedy occurs. In this way he exchanges the boyish pastimes of the cinema and the novelty shop in the first part of the story for the more serious experience in the slum pub. He is not a qualified observer, for he becomes drunk, sick, and helpless; and the older reporter tells him, in an odd conclusion, that the story which has just been narrated has certain confused details; but he is still naïvely determined to put all the things the older reporter has shown him into a story.

Some of the stories have a note of personal futility and inadequacy which conspires with their prevailing comic tone to produce penetrating irony. The inferior boy who is the hero of "Extraordinary Little Cough" is bullied and mocked. But he turns his shy habit of running away when girls appear into a feat; for, while the other boys are idling with the girls and yielding to romantic illusions, he runs the five miles of beach. As he falls to the ground exhausted at the end of the story, it is clear that he has risen nobly to a challenge while the others have ended in frustration and petty animosities. The two boys who go for a country hike in "Who Do You Wish Was With Us?" feel they are escaping their town lives in the freedom of the country and the beach. But Ray, whose life has been full of terrible family misfortunes, is overtaken by sorrow for his dead brother in the middle of his holiday. The sea turns cold and threatening, and both boys feel that they cannot really escape the life they have fled.

The most powerful story about escape, and the most impressive one in the volume is the last, "One Warm Saturday." Having rejected invitations to join his friends, the young man wanders despondently among the crowds on the beach, finding solace only in the face of a girl whom he flees shyly at first. Ultimately, he again meets the girl, Lou; and, as the two become involved in an oddly mixed group of drinkers, she promises him that his love for her will be fulfilled when they are alone. The party moves from the pub where it began to Lou's room in a huge ramshackle tenement. The young man's anxiety and Lou's demonstrations of affection are intensified, but the others show no signs of leaving. A grotesque frustration occurs when the young man goes out to the lavatory. He is unable to find his way back to Lou's room to claim the night of love she has promised him. Instead, he loses himself in the squalid maze of the tenement and stumbles into the rooms of other lodgers. Ultimately, he gives up and wanders out into the street, having made the "discovery" during his search that all the obscure people of the town share his experience of loss.

Thomas' uncompleted novel, *Adventures in the Skin Trade*, may be considered a continuation of the quasi-autobiography loosely sketched in *A Portrait of the Artist as a Young Dog*, though it is more broadly comic in style than any of the stories. It takes up the narrative of a life much like Thomas' at the point where the last of the stories ends, and its protagonist, Samuel Bennet, is not inconsistent with the wandering, imaginative youths found in the earlier book, though he is much better defined. Thomas seems to have begun *Adventures* in 1940; and, though the first section was published in *Folios of New Writing* in 1941 under the title "A Fine Beginning" and though he was encouraged to continue with it, it remained a fragment at the time of his death.

It may be described as a farce based on the fact that Samuel Bennet and his world are excruciatingly uncomfortable with each other. On the night before he leaves his home town for London, Samuel prepares a number of surprises for his family by breaking his mother's china, tearing up his sister's crochetwork, and scribbling on the lessons that his father, a teacher, is correcting. But he does all this in tears, as if it were a painful necessity; and he says an affectionate farewell the next morning. On the other hand, he is not eager to see London; unwilling to make any decisions or to take any actions, he lingers in the station café until a friend forces him to leave.

The London in which Samuel finds himself is a damp, angular, crowded, eccentric world; and it is both surprising and significant that he likes it as well as he does. The chaos he encounters is well represented by his first stop, a warehouse full of furniture piled up in unlikely heaps which nevertheless serves as living quarters for a number of people. The general technique of *Adventures* is suggested by the locked bathroom with its bird cages where a strange girl makes an attempt on Samuel's virtue in a tub full of used bathwater after drugging him with a drink of cologne. In the book, as in this scene, violent imaginative force explodes in a narrow enclosure filled with ordinary objects and people, toppling them into ludicrous attitudes and combinations. A mundane paraphernalia of Bass bottles, umbrellas, rubber ducks, bootpolish, Worcestershire sauce, and Coca-Cola is juggled into patterns of uproarious private meaning, sometimes by Samuel's imagination, sometimes by the author's. Realism swims in a whirlpool of uninhibited fancy.

If the atmosphere of *Adventure* is found anywhere else, it is in Brinnin's accounts of the social events Thomas attended, where the poet, guided by some motivation of wit or self-dramatization, cunningly introduced chaos. Mr. Allingham observes that the Bass bottle which has become wedged on Samuel's little finger is an enigma. Samuel, noticing that a barmaid looks like a duchess riding a horse, makes the irrelevant reply of "Tantivy" to some remark. But the curious thing is that Samuel, in spite of the hostility and defiance with which he confronts the world, is completely unready for the world's retaliation. As he is pushed and prodded from one place to another, drugged, undressed, bullied, and thrown out of a bar, he experiences terror and confusion. Samuel is too innocent to absorb what he sees. A stumbling, swooning, dreaming source of confusion, he is himself confused, and he seems destined to remain a timid and withdrawn picaro among the sharp and knowing characters who take possession of him. According to Robert Pocock, who discussed *Adventures* with Thomas, the novel was to end with Samuel stripped naked (except, no doubt, for the Bass bottle clinging enigmatically to his little finger), and arrested in Paddington Station.[4]

IV

The two film scripts Thomas completed during the period he was writing for the media of popular entertainment—*The Doctor and the Devils* and *The Beach at Falesá*—are entirely unlike his other work. Both were based on *données,* and they were translations of a given story from one medium to another. They made few demands on Thomas' original gifts, but they did demonstrate that he had unexpected capacities for adapting himself to new forms and for controlling an extended work.

Of the two, *The Doctor and the Devils* is by far the more interesting and successful. The idea for filming the story of the murderers, Burke and Hare, who supplied the early anatomist, Robert Knox, with corpses for dissection, was that of Donald Taylor. Taylor, after some research, wrote a narrative of these episodes; and he commissioned Thomas, then an employee of his Strand Film Company, to write the script. This was the beginning of an odd history. Thomas' script, completed and put into proof by 1947, was not published until 1953. In 1961 Callum Mill rewrote it as a stage play, produced it in this form at the Citizens' Theatre in Glasgow in 1961, and played the role of Dr. Rock. The play was performed a second time at the Edinburgh International Festival in 1962, where Mill staged it for performance "in the round" at the Assembly Hall. The film itself has never been produced.

The effectiveness of Thomas' script is due largely to its accounts of the low haunts of Edinburgh (which is, however, never identified by name), the curious characters found there, and their deeds of violence. The stage directions are cast in a considered prose of far greater finish and vigor than is strictly necessary. Some of them seem to call for inappropriate emphasis, but others display a creative and original approach to photographic possibilities. It is clear that Thomas found the cinematic idiom of concrete imagery entirely congenial. He is both resourceful and subtle in devising visual counterparts for ideas of his own and for the thoughts of his characters. The murder of Jennie Bailey is predicted by a shot showing Fallon, her murderer, unconsciously letting the drink from his bottle pour over her skirt during a carouse. While a student is drawing her corpse, her hand, opening in a death twitch, drops two pennies to the floor. The scenes in the pubs and the parties in the lodging house kept by Fallon and Broom, where they trap and murder old derelicts for Dr. Rock's dissecting table, present a great deal of this specific and telling detail.

The chief character, Dr. Rock, is a figure who resembles Faust or Paracelsus: he is an intellectual devoted to his discipline who is indifferent to ordinary human values. The actual Dr. Knox gave Thomas some of the rudiments of Dr. Rock's character; he was an effective orator and a dandy, and the figure in Thomas' script retains these qualities. Rock defends his practice of accepting bodies obtained by "Resurrectionists" on the ground that the legal limitation of using only bodies from the gallows for dissection is too restrictive. One of his weaknesses as a character is his universal and unfailing contempt; he despises his colleagues, the poor, the government that ignores their needs, and nearly everyone to whom he speaks. Yet he proclaims that he is in the service of mankind; and, when the murders are discovered, the other doctors, whom he has bitterly criticized, unite to defend him.

Rock is the center of the script's moral conflict. Believing not only that any means are justified in the pursuit of his science but that the lives of the poor and immoral people upon whom Fallon and Broom prey are not worth living, he accepts the bodies silently, even though he knows they have been murdered. When the truth becomes known, he is ostracized; and for a few sequences Rock has the odd aspect of an inverted Dr. Stockmann of *An Enemy of the People*: he stands alone against society in defense of his moral indifference. But he is brought to a realization of his crime at the end, when a child is frightened at hearing his name; he then learns that he has become a figure of horror.

In his review, James Agee called *The Doctor and the Devils* the hack work of a man of genius; but the fact that he found much to praise in it showed that he intended to characterize and not to condemn it with this description. He thought that Thomas had made good use of some of the movie devices, that the dialogue was "playable," and that the script showed that Thomas "could not work for money without also working with love."

This observation is not, unfortunately, supported by *The Beach at Falesá*, a script far inferior to *The Doctor and the Devils*. *The Beach* was written in 1948 for Gainsborough Pictures; like the earlier one it was never produced, and it was not published until 1959, when it appeared in *Harper's Bazaar*. A filming of a story by Robert Louis Stevenson, it has to do with an island in the South Seas dominated by a merchant who exploits the superstition of the natives to interfere with the business of a rival trader. It offers some interesting local color and some humor drawn from the life of white men in the tropics. There is a good scene in which the English hero sets up housekeeping with his native wife and tries to explain how his new household differs from his own home; but he finally surrenders to her naïveté, gives up the attempt, and contents himself with amusing her. In general, however, the script aims at melodrama, violent physical action in the form of fist fights, and spookiness. There are few signs that Thomas tried to make anything serious or original of the assignment.

Thomas' last completed work, *Under Milk Wood*, had a long gestation, for he first thought of writing something like it in 1945, as an expansion of the subject of "Quite Early One Morning," a description of a Welsh village he had read on the radio during one of his programs. The original plan, according to Daniel Jones, was to have the town full of queer individualists defend its sanity at a trial; but, upon hearing a description of a sane town from the prosecutor, the inhabitants decide instead to shut themselves off from the outside world. After writing about half of the play, calling it *The Town Was Mad*, Thomas changed his mind about this structure. In the summer of 1951 he read some parts of the play—then called *Llareggub Hill*—to Brinnin; and in 1952 he published a selection closely resembling the first half of the final version in *Botteghe Oscure* as *Llareggub: A Piece for Radio Perhaps*.

When Brinnin suggested in September of 1952 that the play

might serve as a program for the series of American readings they were planning, Thomas was encouraged to complete it. It was listed in the program of the Poetry Center for performance in May, 1953; Thomas wrote in March that he would not be able to complete it before leaving for America but that he would bring the manuscript with him. He continued work on it up to the very day he first read it as a solo performance at the Fogg Museum in Cambridge Massachusetts, on May 3, 1953. The reaction to this premiere was enthusiastic; according to Brinnin, it gave Thomas confidence in his ability to write drama. A first group reading was given at the Poetry Center on May 14; its effect was extraordinary, and there were fifteen curtain calls. Thomas continued to revise the play and to add to it through the ensuing performances, until the weeks just before his death. The play opened the Poetry Center's program in September, 1953, and was first performed in Britain as a broadcast on January 25, 1954.

In spite of its effectiveness, *Under Milk Wood,* like most of Thomas' writing about Wales, is essentially slight; its main assets are charm, exuberance, and mischievousness. Thomas took advantage of the radio-play form to give his work a reality that was as disembodied as possible; apart from the town itself and the well-marked progress of the day from morning to nightfall, there are few suggestions of time or place. There is no plot. The microphone simply makes a number of tours of the various inhabitants of the town at different hours of the day, guided on one occasion by the postman, to hear of their dreams, memories, and daily lives. There are no distinctions between the voices of characters and narrators, the speeches of the living and the dead; or among dreams, thought, and *viva voce* dialogue. In form—or, rather, in formlessness—its closest analogue is the Night-Town chapter of Joyce's *Ulysses;* but the nightmare violence and the horror of Joyce's chapter are supplanted by domestic comedy, cheerful lechery, and wistful memories of episodes of affection that are only incidentally sinful.

The comic vitality of *Under Milk Wood* suggests that Thomas, with his sense of humor, his eye for detail, and his love of humble people, might have done work reminiscent of Dickens.

But the humor of *Under Milk Wood* is not an end in itself, but a means of emphasizing the theme, the sacredness of human attachments. Thomas advances a persuasive claim to respect for the sinful, eccentric, and even ludicrous loves that spring up in ordinary lives by investing them with comedy and pathos. This effect begins with the speeches of Captain Cat's drowned shipmates rehearsing the pleasures of their lives: ". . . we shared the same girl once. . . . come to a bad end, very enjoyable." This irresistible style of defense for whatever human beings may come to care for is continued with the dreams of Miss Price, the dressmaker, and Mog Edwards, the draper, whose love for each other never progresses beyond correspondence; with the love between the rowdy Cherry Owen and his wife; with Captain Cat's memories of Rosie Probert; with the Reverend Eli Jenkins' paean to the town and Wales generally; and with Polly Garter's memory of Willy Wee, the one man among all her lovers for whom she cared the most. The more delusive and insubstantial these affections are, the more tenderly does Thomas treat them.

Under Milk Wood turns sharply away from anything resembling mysticism. It reflects the conclusion Thomas had reached in 1951 that "The joy and function of poetry is, and was, the celebration of man, which is also the celebration of God."[5] Thus, it can be seen as the last of Thomas' hymns of praise for the world of man's experience and its Creator. His early mystic poems had mingled the material world and its divine source in a dark, chaotic unity. In his later poems, the landscapes, animals, and people are treated as if they were taking part in a grave and radiant ceremonial; the sense of relation with divine energy has retreated, but its immanence is felt everywhere. In *Under Milk Wood*, with its loving depiction of people who would ordinarily be considered weak or foolish, Thomas continues to pursue this obscure joy.

V

Alfred Kazin has attributed the great popularity Thomas enjoyed in his lifetime to the fact that his resonant, passionate verse offered an alternative to the cool ironies of his contemporaries. Certainly the poets dominating the early 1930's, when *18 Poems* and *Twenty-Five Poems* were published—W. H. Auden, C. Day Lewis, Louis MacNeice, and Stephen Spender— differed from Thomas in two important respects. They were men who responded sensitively to social and historical condi- tions, and they were—with the exception of Spender—primarily poets of wit and intellect. They frequently dealt with themes related to the Depression, the Spanish Civil War, and the threat of World War II, and even their lyrics of personal dis- quiet are touched with an awareness of general conditions. As Auden wrote in his poem about the outbreak of the war, "September 1, 1939":

> Waves of anger and fear
> Circulate over the bright
> And darkened lands of earth,
> Obsessing our private lives. . . .

Even in their pessimism, these poets usually maintained a tone of civilized urbanity and a sense of decorum. Although they often took up the cause of the outsider or the proletarian, they expressed themselves in verse of an aristocratic, intellec- tual, and ironic temper.

However, there were dissidents among the young writers of the time who, like Thomas, favored a return to some of the values of Romanticism. By the mid-1930's, Auden, whose first book of verse had been published in 1930, was regarded by some as cold, brittle, and superficial; new sources of feeling for poetry were being sought in myth, religion, and the subconscious. Ten- dencies resembling those of Thomas' poetry and early stories were found in Surrealism, which began to attract the attention of English writers and artists at this period. David Gascoyne, the only English poet fully committed to Surrealism, wrote *A Short Survey of Surrealism* in 1935, and in 1936 his book of Surrealist verse, *Man's Life Is This Meat,* was published by the Parton Bookshop, which had supported the publication of *18 Poems* two years earlier. Thomas attended the International Surrealist Exhibition held at the Burlington Gallery in 1936, and entered far enough into the spirit of it to carry a cup of tea made of boiled string which he offered to passers-by. Although he was critical of Surrealist theory in the "*Manifesto*" of 1951, the fantastic stories collected in *The World I Breathe* (which were written in the 1930's) certainly share the Surrealist spirit. Thomas' mythic qualities and Romantic egoism also harmonize with the aims of a later literary movement of the 1930's, the New Apocalypse.

Thomas' poetry may legitimately be considered a manifestation of the Neo-romantic stirrings of his time, but it has older and more illuminating affinities as well. Critics writing on Thomas have had much to say about influences and parallels, and it has been shown that he has something in common with nearly every good poet, even those as different from him as Shakespeare and Pope. Thomas' own casual statement on the subject was that he was open to the influence of any writers he might be reading, and his purposely indiscriminate list reads: "Sir Thomas Browne, de Quincey, Henry Newbolt, the Ballads, Blake, Baroness Orczy, Marlowe, Chums, the Imagists, the Bible, Poe, Keats, Lawrence, Anon, and Shakespeare."[6] The most significant name on this list, as Thomas implicitly acknowledges, and as his critics have often pointed out, is that of Blake. Thomas shared with Blake a hallucinatory commitment to the concreteness of what he imagined, and the sort of cosmic awareness that generates myth. Though Thomas' cosmos is far more fragmentary than the one found in Blake's Prophetic Books, it has some of the same energies, gigantic deities, and above all, the same "fearful symmetry" of balanced patterns formed by opposing forces.

Much has been said, also, about the religious or visionary aspect of Thomas' poetry, the quality he shares with Vaughan, Hopkins, and Yeats, as well as with Blake. In general, the critics have adopted one of two opposing points of view. One group thinks of Thomas as a religious poet who wrote, as he said in his introductory note to the *Collected Poems*, "for the love of man and in praise of God." T. H. Jones believes that the main poems of *Deaths and Entrances* clearly exhibit a Christianity that is disguised, but still detectable in the rhetoric of the earlier poems. G. S. Fraser finds in the "Altarwise . . ." sequence a "current of orthodox Christian feeling—feeling rather than thought" which became increasingly noticeable in Thomas' later work. W. S. Merwin's essay, "The Religious Poet" is probably the most cogent statement of this view. Merwin considers Thomas' work a "poetry of celebration," whose universe originates in love and remains suffused with it. It is natural, adds Merwin, that Thomas should have proceeded from lyric to dramatic modes, for the faith developed in the introspections of the earlier poems is revealed, in the later ones, in the form of an increasingly inclusive sense of the orderliness of the external world.[7]

If Thomas said that he wrote "in praise of God," he also said, at another time, that he meant to write "poems in praise of God's world by a man who doesn't believe in God."[8] This statement, which seems more careful than the one in the introduction to *Collected Poems,* also seems intended to strike a note of qualified faith. Many, perhaps most of Thomas' critics, feel that his poetry, in spite of its Biblical allusions, its use of Christian myth and symbolism, and its ardent declarations of faith is not, in the final analysis, expressive of religious belief. "It would be ridiculous," wrote Francis Scarfe in one of the earliest analyses of the "Altarwise . . . " sequence, "to claim Thomas for any church."[9] And a recent critic, Ralph Maud, commenting on Thomas' allusions to God in "Over Sir John's hill" and the projected, but uncompleted "In Country Heaven," observes: "Thomas' God does nothing to alleviate the absurdity of the position of rational man in an irrational universe; Thomas' God does nothing to explain death in terms of higher values. As the eternal sympathetic spectator, He simply weeps, offering none of the usual consolations."[10]

The differences of opinion on this point among the critics are at least partly due to different notions of what is meant by "religion." Thomas is certainly concerned with such religious problems as the nature of the creator, the relation of man to his universe, and, particularly, the enigma of death. Also, his verse depends upon mystic perception, intuitions about the cosmos, and even upon such specifically Christian doctrines as atonement, immortality, and salvation. But his ideas about these things are personal, naïve, and, as we have said earlier, primitive. In spite of his use of conventional religious terms and symbols, Thomas' subject is really the primordial world view of the savage. It includes miracle, anthropomorphism, and pantheism, but offers no morality, no doctrine, no communal feeling. Thomas' religious symbolism, says Giorgio Melchiori, "is only a metaphorical means of expression of the poet's personal thought; it contributes to the creation of that personal myth which seems to be the real aim of his poetry."[11]

Thomas is a craftsman of language as well as a visionary. Though he explicitly denied that Joyce had influenced him, he is properly seen as one of the line of verbal experimenters of which Joyce is the most prominent member. We have already examined Thomas' imaginative use of words, and it is interesting to recall that he enjoyed reading old copies of the magazine *transition,* that museum of exploration in language. What Thomas has in common with Lewis Carroll, Hopkins, Joyce, and Cummings is the urge to probe the disparity between conventional language and the fruits of perception. Thomas, like the others, devised more or less systematic means of entering the virgin ground between language and experience. He followed Hopkins' example in discovering new reserves of expression in the sound of language, and in coining neologisms to convey the truths of private anguish and joy in nature. And, like Joyce, he practiced the art of doubling or trebling thicknesses of meaning, so that language becomes startlingly germane to its subject.

Thomas is a striking figure, however, not because of the debt he owed to other poets, but because of his undeniable originality. As we have seen, his ideas were not exceptional. He took his intuitions as they came to him, without trying to refine or reshape them, but he spent great effort on the elaboration of rhetorical resources. There are styles of primitive art that display this combination of the simple and the intricate. They offer no defenses against tribal fears and passions, but instead express them in the tangled pattern of a woven shield or the carved involutions of a witch doctor's mask. Thomas' verse strangely resembles objects of this kind. It embodies elemental, unformed feelings that usually lie below the threshold of consciousness in a technique so practiced and accomplished that it gives the illusion of issuing from long, secure traditions foreign to impatient modern craftsmanship. The result is a unique impression of double remoteness, a union of barbaric subject with an arcane, sophisticated style that is perhaps the distinctive quality of Thomas' art.

Notes and References

Chapter One

1. In *Encounter,* January, 1954, pp. 9-10. Reprinted in *Dylan Thomas: The Legend and the Poet,* ed by E. W. Tedlock, Jr. (London, 1960), pp. 15-18, and in *A Casebook on Dylan Thomas,* ed. by John Malcolm Brinnin (New York, 1960), pp. 279-82.
2. The chronology of composition and publication of Thomas' poems is tabulated in "Dylan Thomas' 'Collected Poems,' " by Ralph Maud, *Publications of the Modern Language Association,* LXXVI, 3 (June, 1961), 292-97. A fuller chronology, giving dates of composition and publication of all Thomas' work, is given in Maud's *Entrances to Dylan Thomas' Poetry* (Pittsburgh, 1963), Appendix I, pp. 121-48.
3. Quoted in "Talks with Dylan Thomas" by Harvey Breit, *Casebook,* p. 195.
4. Ralph Maud, "Dylan Thomas' First Published Poem," *Modern Language Notes,* LXXIV (February, 1959), 117-18.
5. Tedlock, p. 18.
6. Edith Sitwell, "Four New Poets," *London Mercury,* XXXIII (February, 1936), pp. 383-90
7. Dylan Thomas, *Letters to Vernon Watkins* (London, 1957); p. 36 (February 7, 1938).
8. John Malcolm Brinnin, *Dylan Thomas in America* (Boston, 1955), p. 126.
9. *Letters to Vernon Watkins,* p. 38 (March, 1938).
10. Thomas, "Poetic Manifesto: A Manuscript," *Texas Quarterly,* IV (1961), 4, pp. 44-53. Introduction by Richard Jones. Thomas' manuscript is photographically reproduced. The quotation appears on page 8 of the manuscript.

11. Augustus John, "The Monogamous Bohemian," *Adam International Review*, No. 238, 1953 (Dylan Thomas Memorial Number), pp. 9-10.

12. *Letters to Vernon Watkins*, p. 27 (July 15, 1937).

13. *Ibid.*, p. 112 (August 28, 1941).

14. "Three Poems," *Quite Early One Morning* (New York, 1954), p. 180.

Chapter Two

1. Thomas, "Poetic Manifesto: A Manuscript," pp. 44-53. The quotation is on page 2 of the facsimile manuscript.

2. *Ibid.*, p. 1.

3. *Ibid.*, p. 2.

4. W. T. Stace, *Time and Eternity* (Princeton, 1952), p. 74.

5. G. S. Fraser, *Vision and Rhetoric* (London, 1959), p. 227.

6. Elder Olson, *The Poetry of Dylan Thomas* (Chicago, 1954), p. 20.

7. *Adventures in the Skin Trade and Other Stories*, (Norfolk, Conn., 1955), p. 117. This passage and its significance as a description of Thomas' universe has also been noted by Ralph J. Mills, Jr. in "Dylan Thomas: The Endless Monologue," *Accent*, XX (Spring, 1960), p. 122.

8. Ernst Cassirer, *An Essay on Man* (Anchor Edition), p. 108.

9. Thomas E. Connolly, *Explicator*, XIV, 5 (February, 1956), No. 33.

10. "Six," dated August 29, 1933 in August, 1933, Notebook, Lockwood Memorial Library, University of Buffalo. The manuscript notebooks cited are in this collection. For an account of their contents, see Ralph Maud, *Entrances to Dylan Thomas' Poetry*, Appendix I, "Chronology of Composition," pp. 124-25. "Shiloh's Seed" has been published posthumously as one of "Five Early Poems" by Thomas in *Poetry*, LXXXVII, 2 (November, 1955), pp. 84-90.

11. Philip Wheelwright, *The Burning Fountain* (Bloomington, 1954), p. 164.

12. Quoted in Henry Treece, *Dylan Thomas* (London, 1949), footnote, p. 48. It should be noted that unmoving time is an unexpressed condition of Thomas' poems. When he actually mentions time, as in "When, like a running grave, time tracks

you down," he usually intends the conventional meaning, with conventional associations of decline and decay.

13. The unpublished poems described in this discussion are from the February, 1933, Notebook in the Lockwood Memorial Library.

14. "Poetic Manifesto," p. 6.

15. Introduction to *Letters to Vernon Watkins*, pp. 12-13.

16. John Bayley, *The Romantic Survival* (London, 1957), p. 196.

17. See Olson, "*The Poetry of Dylan Thomas*, pp. 55-59, for a general discussion of Thomas' metaphor.

18. Ernst Cassirer, *Language and Myth* (Dover Publications, n. d.), p. 58.

19. Christine Brooke-Rose, *A Grammar of Metaphor* (London, 1958), p. 203. A discussion of Thomas' metaphor appears on pages 200-203.

20. Frederick Clarke Prescott, *Poetry and Myth* (New York, 1927), pp. 26-27.

21. Quoted in Treece, *Dylan Thomas*, footnote, p. 48.

22. *Ibid.*, pp. 47-48.

23. Ernst Kris, *Psychoanalytic Explorations in Art* (New York, 1952), p. 245. Kris says this type of ambiguity occurs "when the separate meanings function in the process of interpretation as alternatives, excluding and inhibiting each other."

24. "Fifty" (July, 1933), February, 1933, Notebook.

25. "Four," dated February 6, 1933, February, 1933, Notebook.

26. *Adventures in the Skin Trade,* p. 112.

27. Bayley, *The Romantic Survival*, p. 214.

28. Cassirer, *Language and Myth*, p. 33.

29. Quoted in Treece, *Dylan Thomas*, pp. 149-50.

30. Cassirer, *Language and Myth*, p. 55.

31. *Letters to Vernon Watkins*, p. 31 (November 13, 1937).

32. Cassirer, *Language and Myth*, p. 58.

33. Quoted in Treece, *Dylan Thomas*, footnote, p. 48.

34. See Ralph Maud's *Entrances to Dylan Thomas' Poetry*, pp. 5-6 and 160-61, for syllable counts of some poems and related discussion. In checking my count of the syllables in "My hero bares his nerves," readers may find that the lines "And these poor nerves so wired to the skull," and "He holds the wire from this box of nerves" are each one syllable short. Actually, "wire,"

with its long vowel, is nearly, or actually, a dissyllable, and the fact that Thomas counted it as one shows that he was attending to the sound, not the measure, of his verse.

35. In his *Entrances to Dylan Thomas' Poetry*, Maud offers a detailed analysis of this troublesome poem on pages 81-84, and a discussion of its imagery on pages 86-88 and 90-94. Although his comments are very helpful, they leave room for the feeling that the interests of syntax and coherence are somewhat at odds with each other in this poem.

Chapter Three

1. In Treece, *Dylan Thomas*, footnote, p. 48.

2. David Aivaz, "The Poetry of Dylan Thomas," *Hudson Review*, III (Autumn, 1950), 390 ff.

3. For Tindall's discussion, see *A Reader's Guide to Dylan Thomas* (New York, 1962), pp. 37-38.

4. "Poetic Manifesto," pp. 1-2.

5. Maud finds that the attitude toward dreams expressed in these poems has its origin in dreams involving the sexual waste of nocturnal emission and masturbation. See his *Entrances to Dylan Thomas' Poetry*, pp. 72-79, a passage which contains a general discussion of "Our eunuch dreams." As is often the case in Thomas, the imagery, though handled in a strikingly original way, is far from unprecedented. The analogy between waking and sleep on the one hand and faith and doubt on the other occurs, for example, in Browning's "Bishop Blougram's Apology":

> I say, faith is my waking life:
> One sleeps, indeed, and dreams at intervals,
> We know, but waking's the main point with us.

6. "Thirty Seven," dated March, 1934, in the August, 1933, Notebook.

7. See the interpretation of this poem as a psychological and sexual statement by Marshall W. Stearns in "A Critic Interprets a Poem," *Transformation 3* (London, 1945), reprinted as Appendix III of Treece, *Dylan Thomas*, pp. 151-54, and included in Stearns' article, "Unsex the Skeleton," *Sewanee Review*, LII (July, 1944), pp. 424-40.

8. Robert Horan, "In Defence of Dylan Thomas," *Kenyon Review*, VII (Spring, 1945), p. 308.

9. "Twenty Three," dated October 12, 1933, in the August, 1933, Notebook.

10. "Fifty," (July, 1933), February, 1933, Notebook.

11. "Five Early Poems" by Dylan Thomas, *Poetry*, LXXXVII, 2 (November, 1955), pp. 84-90.

12. "Thirty Seven," dated July 1, 1933, in February, 1933, Notebook.

13. "Twenty Two," dated October 5, 1933, in August, 1933, Notebook.

Chapter Four

1. For information about dates of composition, I have depended on the manuscript notebooks in the Lockwood Memorial Library, and also on Maud, *Entrances to Dylan Thomas' Poetry*, Appendix I, "Chronology of Composition," pp. 121-48.

2. See Maud's "Dylan Thomas' *Collected Poems*: Chronology of Composition," *PMLA*, LXXVI (June, 1961), pp. 292-97. Also *Entrances to Dylan Thomas' Poetry*, pp. 122-23.

3. "Twenty One," dated April 1, 1933, in February, 1933, Notebook.

4. "Twenty Six," dated April 22, 1933, in February, 1933, Notebook.

5. "Thirty Eight," dated July 4-5, 1933; published posthumously as one of "Five Early Poems" in *Poetry*, LXXXVII, 2 (November, 1955), pp. 84-90.

6. Quoted in Treece, *Dylan Thomas*, footnote, p. 47.

7. Howard Nemerov, "The Generation of Violence," *Kenyon Review*, XV (Summer, 1953), p. 477.

8. "Two," dated December 18, 1930, in 1930-32 Notebook.

9. Tindall, *A Reader's Guide to Dylan Thomas*, pp. 119-20.

10. "Seventeen" and Eighteen," dated September 25 and September 26, in August, 1933, Notebook.

11. In "Dylan Thomas" by E. Glyn Lewis, pp. 168-85 of Tedlock.

Chapter Five

1. In *Entrances to Dylan Thomas' Poetry*, pp. 144-46, Maud

argues that such internal evidence as the simplicity of the main image shows this to be an early poem.

2. Tindall, *Reader's Guide*, pp. 164-66.

3. Andrews Wanning, "Criticism and Principles," *Southern Review*, VI (Spring, 1941), pp. 792-810.

4. Augustus John, "The Monogamous Bohemian," pp. 9-10.

5. Brinnin, *Dylan Thomas in America*, pp. 106-9, 115-16, 141-44, etc.

6. "Twenty Five," dated April 20, 1933, in February, 1933, Notebook.

7. *Letters to Vernon Watkins*, pp. 30-31 (November 13, 1937).

8. *Ibid*, p. 92.

9. Robert Graves condemned the first five lines of this poem as "nonsense," and offered a prize of a pound to anyone who could interpret them. When a member of the Cambridge English Faculty submitted an explication, Graves found it unsatisfactory. See his footnote to the passage from *The Crowning Privilege* reprinted as "These Be Your Gods, O Israel!" in *Casebook*, p. 165.

10. "Thirty Six" in the February, 1933, Notebook. Undated, but written in the summer of 1933. The final version, dated September, 1938, appears on the facing page.

11. John L. Sweeney, Introduction, Thomas' *Selected Writings* (New York, 1946), pp. xvi-xvii.

12. First noted by Geoffrey Moore in "Dylan Thomas: Significance of His Genius," *Kenyon Review*, XVII (Spring, 1955), 258-77.

13. G. S. Fraser, "Dylan Thomas" in *Casebook*, pp. 53-54. (Reprinted from *Vision and Rhetoric*, London, 1959.)

14. For Olson's discussion of this inappropriate detachment, see his *Poetry of Dylan Thomas*, p. 23 ff. His example is "Among those killed in the dawn raid."

15. G. S. Fraser, *Vision and Rhetoric*, p. 237. (Casebook, p. 54)

Chapter Six

1. See G. S. Fraser's excellent discussion of this group in *Vision and Rhetoric*, pp. 228-231. (Reprinted in *Casebook*, pp. 47-50.)

2. Bill Read, "A Visit to Laugharne," *Casebook*, pp. 269-70.

3. "Three Poems," *Quite Early One Morning*, pp. 177-80.

4. See the syllable count of this poem in Maud, *Entrances to Dylan Thomas' Poetry*, p. 161.

5. For an account of the development of this poem, see Maud, "The *Over Sir John's hill* Worksheets," *Explorations*, VI (July, 1956) pp. 81-83. Some of this information, together with an extended analysis and evaluation of the poem, appears in Maud's *Entrances to Dylan Thomas' Poetry*, p. 103 ff.

6. Tindall, who really favors the view that the Thief is an "unassigned symbol," emphasizes the importance of "falling" in relation to the Thief, and speculates that he may represent death, time, maturation, or "the knowledge that destroys innocence and glory." (*Reader's Guide*, pp. 273-80.) Merwin seems to think he represents "the sense of death" (*Casebook*, p. 65). Maud regards his as death, but one which the girl desires (*Entrances*, p. 114). T. H. Jones thinks he is "God, the bringer of death" (*Dylan Thomas*, Edinburgh and London, 1963, p. 99).

Chapter Seven

1. These three studies of the "Altarwise" sequence are: Olson, *The Poetry of Dylan Thomas*, Chapter 6, "The Sonnets," pp. 63-89; Tindall, *A Reader's Guide to Dylan Thomas*, pp. 126-43; and H. H. Kleinman, *The Religious Sonnets of Dylan Thomas* (Berkeley and Los Angeles, 1963), *passim*. All three rely heavily on the assumption that the sonnets make use of bodies of arcane knowledge, but they are undercut somewhat by Thomas' statement, "Nowhere, indeed, in all my writing, do I use any knowledge which is not commonplace to any literate person" ("Poetic Manifesto," p. 5). On the other hand, it is hard to take this statement seriously when we recall, for example, that in "Before I knocked," Thomas refers to Mnetha, a personage from Blake's Prophetic Books, temporarily stumping William Empson. Thomas did admit the obvious fact that he made much use of the Bible; this supports the authority of Tindall's reading of the sonnets, which ascribes most of the allusions to Biblical sources.

2. Olson, *The Poetry of Dylan Thomas*, p. 87. For a critique and H. H. Kleinman, *The Religious Sonnets of Dylan Thomas Poetry*, pp. 167-69.

3. Tindall, *Reader's Guide*, p. 127.

4. Kleinman, *Religious Sonnets*, p. 12.

5. See Kleinman, *Religious Sonnets*, p. 28, for other connotations of the ladder and p. 41 for its relation to Egyptian myths.

6. Maud, *Explicator*, December, 1955, No. 16.

7. For information about the mandrake, see Kleinman, *Religious Sonnets*, pp. 16-20. Also, Thomas' explication of these lines in Treece, *Dylan Thomas*, pp. 149-50.

8. See Kleinman, *Religious Sonnets*, p. 29, for another construction of this knotty passage.

9. Maud has pointed out that there are two misprints in this section in the New Directions edition of *Collected Poems*. "Shrowd" is a misprint for "shroud;" and the first publication of the poem in *Life and Letters Today* in December, 1935, has the eleventh line reading "Love's *a* reflection of the mushroom features," thus supplying the verb needed to make a sentence of the last four lines. See *Entrances to Dylan Thomas' Poetry*, p. 153.

10. Conrad Aiken's review of *The World I Breathe*, "A Rocking Alphabet," *Poetry*, LVI (June, 1940), p. 160.

11. The sources referred to in this paragraph are: Marshall W. Stearns, "Unsex the Skeleton," *Sewanee Review*, LII (Summer, 1944) 424-40 (also in Tedlock pp. 113-31); an excerpt from *Auden and After* by Francis Scarfe published in the *Casebook*, pp. 21-33 (the point about Mary is found on p. 28); and Tindall, *Reader's Guide*, p. 139.

12. James Thomson, "The City of Dreadful Night," lines 411-13. Kleinman's footnote reference to this passage is on page 144.

13. W. S. Merwin, *Casebook*, p. 65.

14. See Tindall, *Reader's Guide*, p. 248, Olson, *The Poetry of Dylan Thomas*, pp. 24-25, and Glauco Cambon, "Two Crazy Boats," *English Miscellany*, VII (1956), pp. 251-59.

15. Horace Gregory, "The Romantic Heritage of Dylan Thomas," *Casebook*, p. 134.

16. Shelley, "Alastor," lines 505-508.

Chapter Eight

1. Thomas' book reviews and miscellaneous journalism are listed in *Dylan Thomas: A Bibliography* by J. Alexander Rolph (London and New York, 1956). His unpublished prose work, scripts written for film documentaries, and unpublished pieces read

on broadcasts are listed in Maud, *Entrances to Dylan Thomas'
Poetry*, Appendix I, "Chronology of Composition," pp. 121-48.
2. "Fifty," (July, 1933), in February, 1933, Notebook.
3. "Poetic Manifesto: A Manuscript," pp. 4-5.
4. Robert Pocock, *Adam International Review*, No. 238, 1953,
pp. 30-31.
5. "Poetic Manifesto," p. 9.
6. "Poetic Manifesto," p. 3.
7. The passages referred to in this paragraph are: T. H. Jones,
Dylan Thomas (Edinburgh and London, 1963), pp. 66-67;
Fraser, *Vision and Rhetoric*, p. 224; and Merwin's essay in
Casebook, p. 60 and p. 64.
8. Quoted by Brinnin in *Dylan Thomas in America*, p. 128.
9. Scarfe, *Auden and After*, 1942. Reprinted in *Casebook*, p. 29.
10. Maud, *Entrances to Dylan Thomas' Poetry*, p. 112.
11. Giorgio Melchiori, *The Tightrope Walkers* (London, 1956),
p. 231.

Selected Bibliography

PRIMARY SOURCES

18 Poems (London: The Sunday Referee and Parton Bookshop, 1934).

Twenty-five Poems (London: J. M. Dent, 1936).

The World I Breathe (Norfolk, Connecticut: New Directions, 1939).

The Map of Love (London: J. M. Dent, 1939).

Portrait of the Artist as a Young Dog (London: J. M. Dent and Norfolk, Connecticut: New Directions, 1940).

New Poems (Norfolk, Connecticut: New Directions, 1943).

Selected Writings. Introduction by John L. Sweeney (New York: New Directions, 1946).

Deaths and Entrances (London: J. M. Dent, 1946).

Twenty-Six Poems (London: J. M. Dent and New York: New Directions, 1950).

In Country Sleep (New York: New Directions, 1952).

Collected Poems, 1934-1952 (London: J. M. Dent and Norfolk, Connecticut: New Directions, 1952).

The Doctor and the Devils (London: J. M. Dent and Norfolk, Connecticut: New Directions, 1953).

Quite Early One Morning (New York: New Directions, 1954).

Under Milk Wood (Norfolk, Connecticut: New Directions, 1954).

Adventures in the Skin Trade (Norfolk, Connecticut: New Directions, 1955).

A Prospect of the Sea (London: J. M. Dent, 1955).

A Child's Christmas in Wales (Norfolk, Connecticut: New Directions, 1955).

Letters to Vernon Watkins. Introduction by Vernon Watkins (London: J. M. Dent and Faber and Faber, 1957).

The Beach at Falesá (New York: Stein and Day, 1963).

Selected Bibliography

1. Bibliographies

(Since the present listing is highly selective, the reader in search of more complete coverage is urged to consult the following longer bibliographies.)

Brinnin, John Malcolm. "Bibliography," pp. 295-310 in *A Casebook on Dylan Thomas* (New York: Little, Brown, 1960). Lists many articles and reviews, as well as material in book form.

Huff, William H. "Appendix C. Bibliographies of Works by Thomas and Works About Thomas," pp. 102-46 in *The Poetry of Dylan Thomas* by Elder Olson (Chicago: University of Chicago, 1954). Gives year-by-year listings and is particularly useful for Thomas' uncollected publications.

Rolph, J. Alexander. *Dylan Thomas: A Bibliography* (New York: New Directions, 1956). A thorough descriptive bibliography, listing uncollected publications and reprints and giving invaluable "literary biographies" of the poems, recording all their appearances, with analyses of variants and misprints.

2. Studies

Adams, Robert M. "Taste and Bad Taste in Metaphysical Poetry: Richard Crashaw and Dylan Thomas," *Hudson Review*, VIII (Spring, 1955), 61-77. Defends the "Altarwise by owl-light" sequence against the charge that it is in bad taste by arguing that metaphysical poetry usually expresses states of mind that conflict with conventional notions of decorum.

Aivaz, David. "The Poetry of Dylan Thomas," *Hudson Review*, III (Autumn, 1950), 382-404. Analyzes some of Thomas' uses of imagery in an illuminating fashion, and shows how the concept of "process" occupies a central position in his poetry.

Arrowsmith, William. "The Wisdom of Poetry," *Hudson Review*, VI (Winter, 1954), 597-604. Argues that Thomas' primitiveness and obsession with "process" prevent him from achieving a coherent moral view. Reprinted (in part) in *Casebook*, pp. 99-101.

Bayley, John. *The Romantic Survival* (London: Constable, 1957). The chapter on Thomas is an interesting discussion of his novel uses of language and metaphor.

Berryman, John. "The Loud Hill of Wales," in *The Kenyon Critics*, ed. John Crowe Ransom (Cleveland: World Publishing Co., 1951), 255-59. Notes the significance of Thomas' peculiar and repetitive vocabulary, draws attention to his technical resources, and perceptively enumerates the difficulties of his style. Reprinted from *Kenyon Review*, Autumn, 1940.

Brinnin, John Malcolm. *A Casebook on Dylan Thomas* (New York: Crowell, 1960). An important selection of critical comments and reminiscences reprinted with ten of Thomas' poems.

———. *Dylan Thomas in America* (Boston: Atlantic-Little, Brown and Co., 1955). A vivid narrative of the last years of Thomas' life, particularly his American tours, most of it drawn from the author's first-hand observations.

Brook-Rose, Christine. *A Grammar of Metaphor* (London: Secker and Warburg, 1958). Thomas' poetry serves as one of the sources of examples in this interesting study. Many of his images are carefully analyzed, and there are some acute general observations about his style.

Cambon, Glauco. "Two Crazy Boats: Dylan Thomas and Rimbaud," *English Miscellany*, VII (1956), 251-59. Points out common themes and other affinities in the two voyages, and asserts that Thomas' poem, in declaring that poetry and actuality must be merged, has a more positive conclusion than Rimbaud's.

Evans, Oliver. "The Making of a Poem (I): Dylan Thomas' 'Do not go gentle into that good night,' " *English Miscellany*, VI (1955), 163-73; and "The Making of a Poem (II): Dylan Thomas' 'Lament,' " *English Miscellany*, VII (1956), 242-49. Studies of drafts and revisions, illustrated by photographs of manuscripts.

Fraser, G. S. *Vision and Rhetoric* (London: Faber and Faber, 1959), pp. 211-41. After a general account of Thomas' attitudes and poetic world, this passage follows his career volume by volume, differentiating the various stages of his development from each other. Reprinted in *Casebook,* pp. 34-58.

Horan, Robert. "In Defence of Dylan Thomas," *Kenyon Review,* VII (Spring, 1945), 304-10. A spirited defense of Thomas' freedom of imagination, describing his mysticism as a poetic rather than a metaphysical resource. In conceding that his multiple images sometimes interfere with the clarity of Thomas' early poetry, Horan makes some valuable comments about Thomas' rhetorical methods.

Huddlestone, Linden. "An Approach to Dylan Thomas," *Penguin New Writing* No. 35 (1948), 123-60. One of the best of the early analyses of Thomas' work, and a good account of the Christian element in his poetry.

Jones, Richard. "The Dylan Thomas Country," *Texas Quarterly,* IV (Winter, 1961), 34-42. A description of Laugharne and scenes related to Thomas' work. There is also an assessment of the influence on his poetry of the attitude toward language found among the country people.

Kazin, Alfred. "The Posthumous Life of Dylan Thomas," *Atlantic Monthly,* CC (October, 1957), 164-68. Speculates on Thomas' character in an exceptionally penetrating and plausible manner, and offers some explanations both for his popularity and his attitudes.

Kleinman, H. H. *The Religious Sonnets of Dylan Thomas* (Berkeley and Los Angeles: University of California Press, 1963). A study of sources and analogues which probably overestimates Thomas' erudition.

Korg, Jacob. "Imagery and Universe in Dylan Thomas' *18 Poems,*" *Accent,* XVII (Winter, 1957), 3-15. A study of the "key images" found in Thomas' first book of verse.

Maud, Ralph. "The *Over Sir John's hill* Worksheets," *Explorations,* VI (July, 1956), 81-83. A study of imagery and vocabulary in the light of revisions and cancellations found in preliminary drafts.

———. *Entrances to Dylan Thomas' Poetry* (Pittsburgh: University of Pittsburgh Press, 1963). Valuable analyses of Thomas' methods and style illustrated by thorough explications of representative poems. It contains a chronology of the poems based on a study of the manuscripts, and an appendix on textual cruxes.

Merwin, W. S. "The Religious Poet," *Adam International Review,* 1953. Places Thomas as a religious poet bent on celebrating such realities as the wonder of creation, the terror of death, and the love of God. Reprinted in *Casebook,* pp. 59-67.

Miles, Josephine. *The Primary Language of Poetry in the 1940's* (Berkeley and Los Angeles: University of California Publications in English), Vol. XIX, No. 3, 1951, 383-542). Thomas is one of the poets whose vocabulary is studied in this analysis of word frequencies.

Mills, Ralph J., Jr. "Dylan Thomas: The Endless Monologue," *Accent,* XX (Spring, 1960), 114-36. A synthesis of the views of time, death, and poetry found in the early poems, and their modifications in later poems.

Morton, Richard. "Notes on the Imagery of Dylan Thomas," *English Studies,* XLIII (June, 1962), 155-64. Applies a distinction between "archetypal," or generally intelligible, and "artificial," or specialized, images to Thomas' poetry, and examines changes in his use of imagery.

Olson, Elder. *The Poetry of Dylan Thomas* (Chicago: University of Chicago Press, 1954). A sensitive interpretation of Thomas' mysticism and rhetoric, giving valuable keys to his symbols and uses of language. There are a number of illuminating paraphrases. It includes a special chapter of exegesis on the "Altarwise by owl-light" sequence, a glossary of special terms, and a bibliography by William H. Huff.

Stearns, Marshall W. "Unsex the Skeleton: Notes on the Poetry of Dylan Thomas," *Sewanee Review,* LII (July, 1944), 424-40. Reprinted in Tedlock, *Dylan Thomas.*

Tedlock, E. W. Jr. *Dylan Thomas: The Legend and the Poet. A Collection of Biographical and Critical Essays.* (London: Heinemann, 1960).

Tindall, William Y. *A Reader's Guide to Dylan Thomas* (New York: Noonday Press, 1962). For each of Thomas' poems Tindall gives a thoroughgoing, resourceful, and detailed explication, as well as references to other comments. The introduction surveys the criticism, and discusses influences and techniques.

Treece, Henry. *Dylan Thomas: "Dog Among the Fairies"* (London: Lindsay Drummond, 1949). The first book-length study. It attempts to place Thomas with relation to contemporary influences, and has accurate observations about his vocabulary, associative technique, and poetic vision. It also contains some important and much-quoted statements by Thomas.

Index

Index